Auditions
A PRACTICAL GUIDE

Auditions

A PRACTICAL GUIDE

John Hester

THE CROWOOD PRESS

First published in 2012 by
The Crowood Press Ltd
Ramsbury, Marlborough
Wiltshire SN8 2HR

www.crowood.com

British Library Cataloguing-in-Publication Data
A catalogue record for this book is available from the British Library.

ISBN 978 1 84797 333 7

Acknowledgements
Front and back cover, and all illustrative photographs by John Langford of
Otto PM except pages 35, 41, and 98 by Sarah Wynne Kordas.

Special thanks to Tabs Productions, Talking Scarlet and Rumpus Theatre
Company, and all the cast members who appear in the photographs of
their wonderful productions: Julia Binns; Aaron Bixley; James Campbell;
Sam Clemens; Susan Earnshaw; Louise Faulkner; John Goodrum; Anita
Graham; Tessa Hatts; Susie Hawthorne; Karen Henson; Mark Huckett;
Ron Jesheth; Patric Kearns; Sarah Wynne Kordas; Rob Laughlin; Adrian
Lloyd-James; David Martin; Grant Orviss; Clare Owen; Ben Roddy; Heather
Saunders; Jane Shakespeare; Chris Sheridan; Sarah Stanley; George Telfer;
Dominic Vulliamy; Katy Wood and the Nottingham Arts Theatre Youth
Theatre. Much thanks to all my regular colleagues who gave help and
advice, and who have inspired me with their skill and dedication to our job.
Special thanks to Jo Castleton, Mark Hayden, Duncan MacInnes and Jeremy
Lloyd Thomas for ideas and inspiration over a drink!

Dedication
In memory of Mum, Betty Hester, who helped me learn the lines.

Typeset by Jean Cussons Typsetting, Diss, Norfolk
Printed and bound in Singapore by Craft Print International

Contents

Introduction

This book is designed to give a wide overview of auditioning, while at the same time providing an invaluable and practical resource for both professional and amateur performers. It will be especially useful to those who are at the very beginning of their career and contemplating drama school or an alternative form of training for the professional theatre, whether as actors or musical theatre performers. However, it will also be of great value to established performers, who will find not only its particular and detailed instruction extremely useful but will also benefit from the structured instructions given regarding a strategic approach to obtaining auditions, getting work and developing their career.

Along with the obvious focus upon auditioning and securing roles there is also much advice on how performers should conduct themselves when working in order to secure more work. In connection with this, the book also aims to build a philosophical view of the whole process of auditioning, using networking and particular strategies to allow performers to establish their careers and to become more reliant upon a long-term over-view of job finding rather than upon individual auditions.

Chapter 11, 'The amateur alternative', is for those pursuing an amateur rather than a professional career. However, as well as giving particular instruction in this aspect, it also throws the other chapters into context, allowing those for whom theatre is a hobby to access the whole book positively and usefully.

It is suggested that, whatever your reasons for reading this book, you do so sequentially and thoroughly and that you practise all of the suggested exercises in order to make full use of the instruction and advice.

Auditioning can be stressful but, with the right approach, it can also be fun. The book makes clear that developing a robust approach to the process can create a focus for the whole of your learning and development within the auditioning framework. It is hoped that within these pages you will find the education and inspiration needed to be not only an effective audition practitioner but a positive and happy performer too.

OPPOSITE: **Choose your audition song carefully, and ensure that it is right for both your personality and musical talent.**

1 Testing your vocation and considering drama school

This chapter is designed to help those who have yet to begin a theatrical career but are contemplating the first step of applying to a drama school or other type of performer training establishment. If this applies to you then there will be some useful thoughts and information here for you. However, even if you have already passed this stage, you might find the chapter useful in terms of seeking for and executing auditions generally.

THE NEED FOR TRAINING

It is possible to begin a career within the performing arts without undertaking any formal kind of training first, and it cannot be denied that there are a number of highly successful people working today who did not train formally. It is perfectly possible, in theory, to step straight into the profession and take your chance in the job-seeking world of the young performer, alongside those 'graduates' who have recently completed training. However, in practice, to do so will put you at a distinct disadvantage: while it can be accepted that training is not for everyone, in general a lack of formal training will make the task before you even harder than it already is.

Nobody ever stops learning of course and, especially in the early years, working itself is a training

OPPOSITE: **The auditioning process begins with thoughtful and exciting contemplation.**

ground – providing an ever-accumulating wealth of experience and knowledge. However, in order to make the most of this, and to proceed in the right direction, learning the basics in a focused and controlled environment can be essential. There is no person without formal training currently working in theatre who could not, in some way, have benefited and been improved by training had they undertaken it.

TESTING YOUR VOCATION

In general most worthwhile training courses are demanding and require a great deal of dedication and determination to complete. Likewise, the process of securing a place on one is difficult, complex, and testing of both talent and resolve. These facts should not be seen as a deterrent but rather as a huge advantage, as the experience as a whole will not only provide you with the 'tools' you require for a career in the performing arts, but also an excellent way of testing your vocation to embark upon such a career in the first place.

You must be very clear at this stage that wanting, or even longing, to be an actor or musical theatre performer is not enough. The profession you have chosen is an extremely arduous one and will require the investment of your whole life and very being; it is, in every sense of the word, a vocation and you must be sure that it is right for you and (perhaps more importantly) that you are right for it. Many people who drift into theatre without training (and some who do train) bypass the process of testing their vocation and, thus, struggle with the demands of the life they have chosen and ultimately fail. You must avoid this situation at all costs – after all, you would not expect to be able to enter the priesthood, for example, without the Church first thoroughly testing your suitability and desire to do so. Becoming a professional performer should be viewed as being as at least equal to this in its vocational credibility.

Therefore, if you are serious about your chosen career, you should be serious about preparing properly for it, both in terms of gathering the knowledge and skills that you need, and in terms of testing your vocation too. Applying for and undertaking a proper and suitable training course is an ideal way to do both.

You must also make sure that your ambitions are founded upon a firm basis. Having watched a soap opera and thought that you would like to 'have a go' at that is not enough. Make sure that, before you even consider training, you immerse yourself in drama, dramatic literature and performing at all levels, to test thoroughly your ability and commitment.

WHAT TRAINING?

In the past the process of selecting the particular method of training that was right for you was a lot simpler, more straightforward and clear-cut than it is now. In general terms, if you wanted to be an actor you went to drama school; if you wanted to be in musicals you aimed for a musical theatre course at either a drama school or dedicated musical theatre academy; and if you wanted to become a director or teach drama you went to university and got a degree. Not to follow these prescribed paths to achieve your required goal would almost certainly lead to disaster.

Now these lines of distinction are not nearly so clearly drawn and there has been a blurring of

Dreaming of a theatrical career is not enough – you must also be practical, realistic and resourceful.

The *Fame* mentality

There are lots of stoical and inspirational sayings, expressions and metaphors used in the theatrical profession: there need to be in order for performers to be able to survive and battle on in what can be a very hostile world. However, they are not always appropriate or useful in every case and can sometimes be used to avoid the truth or real relevance of a situation. One of these, associated with those whose ambitions ostensibly lie in a theatrical career, is used as a defence against setbacks, put-downs and seemingly negative advice. It is the attitude that however bad things get, however many people tell you that you are wasting your time, and however many rejections you face, you must carry on regardless because you will succeed despite everything and everybody. It is the kind of attitude characteristic of the classic film and television series *Fame*, in which characters at the famous performing arts academy would bravely soldier on against impossible odds and relentless opposition. This made great drama but has also encouraged some unrealistic and ill-founded dreams too.

Of course these sentiments are admirable, useful and, in truth, essential, but only for those whose vocation has been tested, their calling proven and the sufficiency of their talent confirmed. While it is a useful tool for testing your vocation, if used to excess it can become a way of avoiding an obvious truth. Sometimes an experienced and trusted source telling you that you do not 'have what it takes' can be a test to your commitment not to give up too easily but can, in some circumstances, also be a wake-up call to your lack of sufficient talent. This may seem harsh but life is short and, while you must pursue your dreams with vigour and courage, be careful that you do not do so fruitlessly, to the detriment of discovering another vocation to which you may be ultimately much better suited and may be far happier pursuing in the long term.

Reality television talent shows in recent years have added to unattainable ambitions and dreams amongst disillusioned hopefuls: make sure that you are not one of these and listen to the answers that testing your vocation will bring – good and bad! And be wary of the word 'fame' too: if you just want to be famous then there is very likely a lack of proper substance in your wish to become a professional performer anyway.

the definitions between them. There are far more options for prospective performing arts students these days and the choices that they have to make are less rigid and constricting and more open to change and development as the training process progresses. This is in many ways, of course, a good thing, as choice and breadth of opportunity can never be a bad thing generally. However, it has made the procedure a lot more complicated than before and choosing a method of training is now a more tangled prospect than it used to be.

The changes have been principally brought about by a more academic approach to training in general but particularly with regard to actor training. Over the years, more and more drama schools have faced the problem of funding for their students: that is to say, it became increasingly difficult for talented students to secure financial assistance for their courses. For this reason drama schools have increasingly aligned themselves with universities in order to secure more mandatory type funding and this has meant that nearly all drama students now receive degrees at the end of their studies. Therefore the distinction between drama schools and universities offering drama courses is less vivid than it used to be and, in general, there is now also much more of a 'melting pot' of opportunity and choice across the range of acting and musical theatre.

SPOILT FOR CHOICE

Another factor is that there are now far more training establishments to choose from, with liter-

ally hundreds of academies offering professional training in acting and musical theatre. Therefore, not only does the 'student to be' have to choose between a university and drama school type training but, in terms of the latter, she or he now has a bewildering array of possibilities to sift through – and all of this in the light of the fact that any one of them may be very difficult to get into. Do not be fazed by this: despite the ever-increasing complexity of this situation, there is help at hand to untangle to possibilities and make some clear decisions. However, you will need to be systematic, so read on!

ACTING OR MUSICAL THEATRE?

The first decision that you need to make is something of a self-examining one and it is this: are you

Planning your training presents a range of possibilities.

Consider whether your ambitions lie in musical theatre or straight drama.

an aspiring actor or do your ambitions rest within musical theatre?

Before we explore this question further it is important (and interesting) to point out that the divide between these two equally noble sides of the performing profession is not nearly so pronounced as was once the case. One of the major reasons for this is the fact that the level of acting ability within the rank and file of musical performers has improved enormously. In the past this genre has relied upon and demonstrated a high standard of singing and dancing ability, while acting has tended to take second place and be based upon a fairly simplistic, rudimentary approach, rather than the more naturalistic, truthful and sponta-neous technique of those within 'serious' thea-tre. There has been much change here in more recent years and the standard of acting in musicals generally has become better, far more based upon realism, and would generally be much more likely to win the approval of Stanislavski than

before. This, coupled with similarly higher apti-tudes for singing and dancing amongst straight actors has engendered more cross-fertilization between plays and musicals and blurred the distinction between previously distinct wings of the profession.

These changes have, again, brought much greater choices and opportunities to the fledg-ling performer, and have made the initial choice between the two major types of theatre less intimidating and certainly less final – many people who have trained in musical theatre have enjoyed successful careers within straight theatre too, and vice versa. However, although your decision in this area may now not be as irreversible as it might once have been, it is still one that you will need to make prior to, and in terms of, training.

You may be good at, and have a love of, acting and singing and dancing – we have already noted that these talents can often be present in all types of performers. If this is not the case, and your skills and ambitions are directed firmly one way or the other, then the decision will have been made for you and you will instinctively know which way to proceed. But should you find that you possess more of a balance of abilities (indeed, that maybe you are highly talented in all departments), then you will need to evaluate and prioritize more carefully. Yes, you need not worry too much about the finality of your choice but, in practical terms at least, you will need to determine a reasonably firm idea of the direction in which you wish to proceed in order to select the right sort of course and institution for your studies.

Very often it will be your heart that will give you your answer. Examine what really excites you about theatre and being on the stage and, even if you are a consummate actor, singer and dancer, a preference and, indeed, dedication should become clear. Think about why you love theatre. Is it the energy, excitement and buzz of the musical stage or are you more inspired by character work, analysing personality and situation, and emotional exploration. In doing this, ensure that you are honest about your talents and abilities as well. Hopefully, your skill will match your desires and ambition but this is not always the case, and you must be careful to take a good hard look at what you can achieve as well as what you would like to achieve, and always play to your strengths.

Having come to some sort of decision there are decisions to be made in terms of training. Many drama schools (and, indeed, universities) now

Stage school

Many aspiring musical theatre performers (and actors) will have attended, for at least some of their childhood years, a stage school. These are institutions offering the normal aspects of education alongside a full syllabus of theatre arts training – often focusing heavily upon singing and dancing. If you are one of these people, you will need to assess what your theatrical needs are now in terms of further education.

It is possible that you will feel ready to progress out into the profession. Indeed, as most good stage schools have their own theatrical agencies attached, you may have already acquired much professional experience during your school years, and the transition into adult life within theatre may be seamless and natural. On the other hand, you may feel the need to continue your studies at a drama school, university or academy in the same way as everyone else. If this is the case, you will need to ensure that your chosen training path onwards is one that will work in harmony with your experience and skill status and not against it. Particularly in the acting field, many drama schools may feel that you have assimilated too much of a technique and style for them to be able to engineer their own methods into your abilities.

Your attitude will be key here: your mindset may need to be that of one starting from scratch, allowing your accumulated knowledge so far to lay in abeyance for a while so that you can achieve new skills. There should be no fear in this, as your experience and former knowledge will still be there, deep down, ready to emerge later when you have attained a solid framework for their incorporation and harmonization.

Some stage schools, such as the Arts Educational Schools in and around London, are also further education academies as well, and some pupils continue their studies there as students.

offer Musical Theatre as well as Acting courses. In addition to this, there are specialist academies for musical theatre – many of which have a very long and distinguished pedigree. We will explore the opportunities for the musical theatre person, as distinct from actors, in the next chapter.

UNIVERSITY OR DRAMA SCHOOL?

With the move towards a more academic and (perhaps sadly) a less vocational approach towards performer training, has come another choice to make – this time between university and drama school. As you will see shortly, it can be a more obvious decision to make but, nonetheless, there are now more alternatives available than before.

One of the key factors here is the degree situation: where once a 'vocational' training would deprive a performing arts student of this qualification, now it does not. Thus, the worry that a performer would not have 'anything to fall back on' when times were hard, has been largely negated. In the same way that drama schools have become more academic (in order to fulfil their obligations towards a nationally accredited qualification), so have universities become more vocational in approach and, in this way, the gap between the two types of institution has narrowed. Some university courses are now almost fully based upon vocational principles and use very similar structures and formulas to drama schools. In other words, it is now possible (in theory, at least) to train as an actor or musical theatre performer at a university in the same way as it is possible to receive academic

Universities are now more vocational and can provide exciting and stimulating training.

accreditation and 'respectability' at a drama school or musical theatre academy.

However, it is the opinion of this book that you should aim to take the drama school route if at all possible. Many university courses in this area are now extremely good and use very similar techniques, practices and types of teaching personnel to the drama schools. As such they are certainly a very credible alternative but drama school should be your first target. If you are in the position at this stage (as you should be) of having begun the process of testing your vocation and have honestly ensured, to the best of your ability, that you have enough talent, drive and determination to move forward in your quest, then you should do so in the spirit of attempting to pursue the best option first – and this, in most cases, will be drama school.

The reason for this is partly to do with where the finest quality of training probably lies but also about credibility later on in your career – employers will still look for a good drama school credit and a university training (wrongly or rightly) will not hold as much 'clout' or professional respectability on your CV. These comments must be immediately qualified by the further statement that the particular quality, standing and standard of drama school is all-important here (you will be far better going to university than many of the 'lesser' academies around) and we will look at this factor in the next section.

However, there are two other aspects of university training that we should examine prior to this. The first is that, in general terms, it will be easier to secure a place on a good university course than

Modern approaches to training

In the past, most television and film actors were essentially theatre actors who had embraced and moved into these other areas as a matter of course. They were very often consummately attuned to the more subtle and less 'projected' needs of the small and large screen respectively, but would usually consider themselves to be theatre professionals first and foremost.

Today, the screen no longer 'plays second fiddle' to theatre in this way, and a generation of actors is emerging whose experience and skill lie essentially in television at least – if not in film as well. This trend is, of course, directly in line with the decline, sadly, of theatre's popularity, but not, thankfully, its demise. With this has come a new breed of drama school establishments that focus more specifically upon film and television performance than has ever been the case before. For many would-be actors, their ambition inspired and fuelled perhaps more by the screen than the stage, these offer an appealing prospect, and you may wish to consider this when perusing various syllabuses.

On the other hand, if you are truly motivated and 'called' to be a performer it is very likely that the stage will be your first love and, if this is the case, make sure that your choices do not exclude a thorough grounding in stage technique, alongside the currently relevant considerations of camera techniques too. You should be aware that there are many actors today whose careers survive or even flourish on screen but who become lost and technically inadequate when they find themselves upon the stage. If you are a true performer then you will want to avoid this inadequacy at all cost and, therefore, it should be of primary concern in your choice of training.

it will to be accepted for training at a good drama school. Therefore, while this may have been a very poor 'second choice' for someone wanting to enter professional theatre in the past, it is not necessarily so now. Admittedly, second choices are not ideal in any areas of life, and it may well be that, as part of your vocational testing process, repeatedly failing to get into any decent drama school may spell a firm negative answer to this test and it may be time for you to look towards a more appropriate career for you. However, this is not necessarily so in every case, particularly as the competition within the drama school entry market is so strong and the criteria for entry so variously specific from school to school. Therefore, university can, in some specific circumstances, prove an alternative route towards the start of a professional theatre career.

The second aspect is that most drama schools offer a shorter, postgraduate course (usually one year in duration) that can allow you to obtain something of a 'bolt-on' drama school training having studied at university first. This is by no means the perfect solution, but it is certainly something to consider, as it will allow you to benefit from the quality of tuition as well as the kudos of having a good drama school credit to your name. Places on these courses are much fought over too, so this is not an easy alternative by any means, but it is worth keeping in mind as you consider your options. Of course, there is always the problem that having two parts to your training in this way may cause clashes and inconsistencies. Because of this factor it might be worth considering a more academic, and less vocational, drama degree at as good a university as you can, followed by a postgraduate training at a drama school. In this way your 'second choice' may effectively become 'the best of both worlds'.

AIMING HIGH

Having considered all the possibilities and reached the point in your ruminations where you are firm in you determination to train as, and become, a professional performer, you should resolve at the outset to aim high and attempt to secure your first and best option – as previously discussed. It is essential that you grasp the important concept at this stage that some drama schools are better than others (both in terms of quality and reputation within the business) and, although there are a lot to choose from, many are not worth consideration. This situation was largely brought about in the eighties and nineties when, spurred on by the high fees charged by the more established institutions and the large number of potential (and often disappointed) drama students, entrepreneurial people with varying levels of expertise and experience began to set up rival academies in great numbers and of all sizes and types. Many of these were very good and, in some cases, have become recognized and established in their own right. However, many were not but did somehow survive and, with new examples still springing up on a regular basis, there are quite a lot of worthless and pointless courses out there to avoid.

So your first task when applying for a drama school is to find out which are the best ones to aim for. Obviously, this is something of a matter of personal research but help is always at hand – in the next chapter, for example!

2 Applying and auditioning for drama school

WHICH DRAMA SCHOOL?

In Britain there is an organization called the Conference of Drama Schools. This was founded in 1969 and remains a strong association of colleges with the aim of providing quality assured courses of vocational intensity. In addition the *National Council for Drama Training* was set up in 1976, mainly in response to the tide of new schools with dubious and sometimes nefarious credentials, and as a way of establishing a recognizable and measurable standard of excellence. A rigorous and accountable method of accreditation was established, and this allows potential students to observe those establishments providing a service that is not only of a high professional standard but is also recognized within the profession as a worthy and appropriate place at which to train. Obviously the large, older drama schools are included in the list of 'accredited' academies but some of the newer colleges are to be found there too, despite the long and arduous process of obtaining accreditation. Therefore, the *National Council for Drama Training* list of accredited colleges is the best (and probably the only) place to start.

There are similar and equally reliable organizations and associations in other countries too. In the United States there is the *National Association of Schools of Theatre*, which also has a robust accreditation system and provides information and help in order for you to make informed choices about your future education.

Accreditation does not mean standardization in terms of what all the various schools on the list offer, and there is a wide range of different approaches and content within all the accredited courses. Therefore, your next step will be to determine which of the courses you are going to apply for. The broad answer to this question is as many as you can afford (as they all tend to charge fees for auditioning now), but with so many different options on offer (even amongst the accredited ranks) you will need to determine which of them is right, or at least possibly right, for you. Here, as with so many things, research is the vital key – so send for as many prospectuses as you can and study them avidly as well as using the Internet (the colleges all have websites) to build up a detailed picture of what they all have on offer. Try also to seek out people who have direct experiences of the colleges – if not in person then perhaps via Internet chat rooms and other social media.

You will find that there is a diversity of philosophy as well as content to be found. Some drama schools favour a classically based approach; others angle their courses more towards recorded media (such as film and television); others focus their activities upon a particular historical practitioner

OPPOSITE: Working with a good teacher is essential when preparing for an audition.

A good drama school will present the prospective student with a variety of content within their courses.

(such as the extremes of Brecht or Stanislavski). The musical theatre courses that they offer are equally wide-ranging in their approach.

The shortlist of places that you decide to apply for is very much a matter of personal choice and you will find that you are drawn to some courses rather than others. However, your list should generally aim to include good, solid three-year courses that take a professional approach in terms of making sure you are equipped not only to perform well but to conduct yourself properly and effectively out there in the jungle that is the theatrical profession.

THE NUMBERS GAME

It could be that, with relatively little knowledge and experience, you find evaluating all of the various courses on offer a complex and confusing one – even with the help of filtering processes like the accreditation systems in Britain and other coun-

OPPOSITE: Obtaining a place at a good academy is hard but success is rewarding.

tries. On the other hand, it may be that you have a very strong idea of where you wish to study and that your ambitions in this direction are focused and strong. In the same way that you may well have grown up with an overwhelming desire to be a performer, so might you have cherished the idea of attending one particular institution when starting your journey.

If this is the case, then you must certainly apply for an audition at this particular drama school. However, you will not be able to leave it at that: as the entry process for training is so difficult and demanding, you will need a number of options in order to have a reasonable chance of succeeding. In other words, you need to 'spread your bets'. Drama schools operate a call-back system in line with many auditions within the theatre business itself. Applying for and executing just one audition will not only severely limit your chances of a call-back but will give you a very poor sense of how well you did, and how close you came to success if you should fail. Therefore, make sure that you select at least four (or perhaps more) possible courses, so that you have a raft of auditions to which to apply yourself.

THE WAITING GAME

It should be clear to you by now that it is not an easy task that you have set yourself. Because of this you must be prepared for a lengthy process. It may well be that you do not secure a place in your first year of trying. Unfortunately, this is often the case and, if so, you must 're-group' and try again next year. Certainly, if you do get offered a place at a good and established training establishment at your first attempt then you will know for sure that your ambitions have not been ungrounded, and a great deal of your vocational testing will have been accomplished with a very positive result. However, if you do not, this does not necessarily mean that you have been wasting your time, that you are totally unfit for a life in the theatre profession and that you should consider another career forthwith.

It is often the case that a first 'round' of applying and auditioning is needed in order to find your feet and become used to the demands of the auditioning process – to 'warm up'. Many people find that they are successful in their second year of trying, as the experience of the auditions in their first year gives them the edge that they needed and the experience to settle and relax into the process.

So be patient and expect to be in this for the 'long haul'. One of the advantages of applying for several auditions is that, after an unsuccessful first year, you will be able to evaluate your performance realistically and identify where your strengths and weaknesses lie.

For instance, if you apply for and attend around six auditions in a given year and you are turned down straight at all of them, without being awarded any kind of recall, then you will know that there is fundamental work to be done and you need to address significant issues in the way you are approaching the task. This does not necessarily mean that you do not possess sufficient talent and that your quest is in vain (although, in the longer term you must be prepared for this to be the case), but that your auditioning technique needs some work or you are not focusing on the kinds of elements the drama schools are looking for (more of this later). If, on the other hand, you make one or more of the recalls, you will know that you are doing something right and you can then attempt to evaluate what this is and what you now need to do to improve still further. Certainly, if you are offered recalls for all of your applications then you will know for sure that success is not by any means totally elusive and, in such a case, it may well be that another year of living and developing will be all you need to make the difference and secure a place (or choice of places) at the next attempt.

Get help!

As should by now be clear, the initial and ongoing process of auditioning for drama schools and academies is not only arduous, but it also requires a great deal of analysis and development of skill and technique. You should not attempt to do this alone. You will need somebody who can not only steer you in the right direction and hone your abilities, but who will be able to look at you and your situation with an outside eye and advise you reliably and with insight. For this reason you should employ a good teacher to school you in your audition pieces and act as something of a 'personal trainer' for your endeavours. Finding the right tutor is in itself needful of some research and you should select one who has a good reputation for the teaching of acting generally but, more specifically, one who has experience and knowledge both of the theatre business and of professional training. Be careful also that, in selecting someone with experience (and therefore perhaps more on the mature side), they have knowledge of the current drama school auditioning culture and requirements – things may well have changed a bit since they went through the process themselves!

An experienced teacher will be able to help you select audition pieces that are not only acceptable to the various schools but that are right for you and your personality and skills. However, be prepared to pay for this expertise, as private lessons are not usually cheap. Make some enquiries and then look at your budget: it might be that you will not need that many lessons or that they need to be as regular as every single week. Space them out effectively and make good use of every session – it will be money very well spent!

If you start working with a particular teacher and you find either that their expertise or the working chemistry between you is not sufficient then seek an alternative. If they are worthy teachers they should not object to your stopping having lessons if things are not working out, and this is far too important an issue in your life to waste time and money purely for the sake of not offending someone. One of the main criteria for judging a successful relationship with a teacher is simply how much you enjoy the process. If things are good then you should leave each session 'buzzing' and eager for the next session.

THE AGE FACTOR

Most drama schools (unlike many universities) are not always keen to offer places to people straight from school at the age of eighteen. By the very nature of what they are intending to teach you, with the high level of emotional and mental depth that acting requires, this can be restricting or simply too early for effective training. This is not always the case and many actors and musical thea-tre performers have started as students at this age but, generally, you will have more chance when you are a little bit older. For this same reason you should not be put off if you are a potential mature student anyway, as schools will often welcome trainees whose lives and personalities are well established and developed.

This is another reason why this must be seen as a long-term process. You may fail in your first year of trying simply because you are too young or

Be realistic

Although you must be prepared to take your time in this matter, you must also be prepared to be realistic if, having taken time, it becomes obvious that you are not going to succeed. We have established that one year is not usually enough and it could be that three might be needed and appropriate. But, again, evaluation of your situation must come into play. If your second year of trying produces no recalls either, and you have conducted your auditioning process carefully and with help, then it might be time to recognize that this might not be for you. Give yourself plenty of chances but do not waste too much time and expense if, in the longer term, your quest remains fruitless. It may then be the point to start considering other options.

require more experience of life. Remember that as your quest to secure a place on a suitable course develops so will you – not only in terms of ability but also as a person.

GETTING FEEDBACK

Although this would seem to be an obvious necessity in order to progress your auditioning abilities, it is easier said than done. In general drama schools do not offer any reasons or hints as to why they turn potential students down. This is understandable on a purely practical level; they may also feel that things they say and advice they give may be used against them later in our increasingly litigious culture. However, when you are paying a fee for the privilege it can be galling to be rejected without knowing why or, at least, having some pointers for the future. You can, of course, try asking for this information but you are liable to disappointment in the response.

Therefore, you must find other ways of obtaining feedback. Aside from recognizing your need for assistance in this area in terms of tutorial help, you must also start to get a 'feel' for what things are going right and why, and what things (even more importantly) are going wrong and why. This intuition obviously comes with time, practice and experience of auditioning and simply being in the various drama schools and engaging with those people who are auditioning you. Yet, again, we find ample reason why this whole endeavour must be viewed as a considerable time investment and not just a fast and furious dash to success or failure.

PREPARING AN AUDITION FOR DRAMA SCHOOL

So here you are at the beginning of your endeavours to secure a place at an accredited drama school of your choice. You have applied to a good selection of establishments, having fully researched the content and philosophies of the courses they offer first, and you are now beginning to get some audition dates coming through. It is now time to choose and prepare some audition speeches. Obviously there are other areas of this book that can help you with both of these tasks but it will be helpful here to consider some particular requirements for this type of auditioning.

One of the first things to consider is that training

OPPOSITE: **Select your pieces and prepare them carefully.**

establishments do a lot of auditioning and, therefore, see a great many different people performing a plethora of dramatic and comic monologues. Unlike those auditioning people for a job within the profession, there is no form of pre-selection process (they will not be looking at photographs and CVs with a view to short-listing suitable candidates for a particular part) and they must therefore audition all of the many hopefuls who apply each year. You will be doing yourself an enormous favour if you avoid picking too obvious and potentially well used pieces that they may have seen a thousand times before and have become thoroughly saturated and bored with. Try to be as original as you can and select speeches from less well-known plays in order to help them observe you with more refreshed eyes. Avoid the obvious and seek out not necessarily the obscure but certainly the less mainstream and obvious choices. However, a word of caution: do make sure that they are quality pieces and fulfil all the other requirements noted here and elsewhere in this book.

Drama schools do not tend to suggest possible audition pieces, as they are interested to see the selection choices you make, but some of them may provide you with a list of speeches that they particularly don't want you to prepare (either because of the aforementioned repetition aspect or because they deem them unsuitable) and so it is worth checking this with each of the schools that you have applied to.

The most helpful factor when picking and preparing an audition speech for drama school is to focus upon exactly what it is they will be looking for when they watch you perform. Certainly, they will not be looking for polish. They are not particularly interested in the finer details of your technique as this will be their job. Indeed, the less 'made-up' and complete you are as a performer the better, for the easier it will be for them to 'construct' you as performer without huge amounts of deconstruction first. Significant potentially bad habits and highly entrenched methods will tend to put them off for fear of too onerous a task when training you. They want you to provide them with plenty of raw talent and potential, so you need to pick pieces that will show off as much of your potential in this regard as possible. Similarly, your preparation of these pieces must release and demonstrate these ingredients to the full and in the very best and most accessible way.

In thinking about revealing all of these talents and qualities to entice the would-be trainer into wanting to work and shape them, you should remember to do so equally for mind, body and voice. Yes, it is definitely important that you possess a talented heart and mind, but they will also want to see if you can move and what your voice can do as well. So make sure that your audition pieces reveal all of these aspects, avoiding, for example, speeches in which you are too static, and ones that do not show off a reasonable range of both notes and tones in your voice. You will usually be asked to provide two pieces for a drama school audition (although this may vary) and so you will have reasonable scope with which to display your 'wares' with some generosity.

As you rehearse and practise, ensure that you are really focusing on bringing lots of potential within you to the surface. Keep the energy of what you are doing high and do not be afraid to show off a little. Let them see what is there and hide nothing – then it is up to them to decide if they want you or not. Do not get too bogged down with detail and perfection – paint with a broad brush stroke and splash the colour about a bit, so that you really allow the auditioning panel to observe and understand exactly what you are about, both as a person and a performer.

THE INTERVIEW

As well as being asked to perform your audition pieces, a drama school will probably afford you a short interview as well. This might not happen until a recall but, more often than not, it will be part of the first audition. It may be in a separate room or it might take the form of simply asking you to sit down after you have done your speeches for a quick chat. There is a great potential pitfall in your attitude here because it is very easy to (rightly) focus upon the performing aspect of the audition and view the interview (however formal or casual it may be) as something of an 'add-on' and not of too high an importance. On the contrary, the interview is vital, for it is these few moments that will reveal to them your attitude about becoming a professional performer.

They will probably ask you a number of ques-tions, some of which will be generalized and others more specific. However, almost certainly and in every case, the main question that they will want to put to you (in whatever guise it may take) is why you want to become an actor or a musical thea-tre performer. The way you answer this question is vitally important. Remember that it is a vocation that you wish to undertake – you are not apply-ing for a short-term job in a shop or office – and so stating that you have always loved acting since a child, or that people at work think you are a brilliant mimic, or you think that you enjoy pretending to be other people, is not enough by any means. It is most certainly not enough to reply that you are thoroughly fed up with

The interview is all-important and you must expect your vocation to be vigorously interrogated.

your current job, want a change, and have always regretted that your parents discouraged you from going into the theatre when you were younger. Dissatisfaction with your present life is no excuse for contemplating a vocation – it just means you need a change of direction. Contemplating becoming a professional performer requires something more than all of this, and they will want to know that you understand this and possess it – otherwise they will simply suggest that an amateur career will satisfy your cravings just as adequately.

What they will want to know from you is not why you want to be a performer but why you cannot avoid being one – why you have to take this course in your life quite irrespective of what you want to do. In other words, they will need to know that your ambition is not only in your mind but in your heart and soul as well; that it runs through your blood and that, despite all the many reasons why you should not enter the theatre business, doing so will be unavoidable – not a choice but a necessity!

How to convey this is not something that is easy to advise you upon, as each individual will have to find their own unique way of expressing such a deep and profound calling. However, if it is there, you must find a way to express it and it will help you to consider your response to this question very carefully. Indeed, this may in fact be part of your vocation testing, for if the proper answer is not within you in some form then perhaps neither is there a sufficient amount of vocational desire. So be ready for this question as if it were the most important question of your life – it may very well be so!

Those auditioning you may also want to explore whether or not you fully appreciate just how hard a life the theatrical profession can be. No glib responses will suffice in this regard either: you must fully and honestly explore what it is that you are wanting to 'let yourself in for' and

have a substantial response as to why you nonetheless think it is right for you to continue with your ambitions.

REMAINING POSITIVE

There can be no doubt that trying to obtain a place upon an accredited course at a drama school is not, by any means, an easy process. Each year there is an ever-growing number of people who decide that a life in the theatre is one that they must have and embark upon the same quest as yourself. Therefore, the competition is enormous; there will probably be hundreds of applicants for each place available in any given year. We have already noted how such a difficult process will involve you in time and money and that you must be prepared to engage in at least two years of auditioning, facing disappointment and rejection, whilst continually monitoring your improvement and realistically analysing your chances.

However, before you become too depressed or dispirited about the task ahead, there are a couple of factors that may help you to feel more positive about the situation you are facing. For you will need to be positive. Yes, you must be realistic about the enormity of the task you have set yourself, but honest appraisal of yourself and your chances will allow you to be sure that you are doing the right thing. If you are able to continue in certainty of your vocation, talent and dedication, then you should feel that you have earned the right to do so positively and with faith in yourself and your ability to succeed – however hard it may be.

The first of these enlightening and encouraging factors is that many of the hopefuls who will fill the audition lists along with yourself are, in fact, hopeless! When there is a lot of competition for something it is easy to imagine that everybody is absolutely marvellous and much, much better and more likely to succeed than you. In this instance this is just not the case. There will be many very talented and capable contenders for sure, but there will also be many more contenders who do not stand a chance. Remember that anybody can apply for drama school and pay for an audition. Just because they think that they have the necessary talent to pursue their dream does not mean that they actually have it. Many of the would-be performing arts students who pass before auditioning panels will have no idea of what is required of them: many will have not prepared suitably, will have chosen ridiculously inappropriate audition material, will not know their words properly (if at all), have no idea about how to act (or sing or dance), display none of the raw ingredients for training we have talked about and will generally cause those who are auditioning them to take a very deep breath before ruling them out of contention in double quick time. As long as you have made sure that you are not one of these, and that you have culti-vated true and founded ambitions, then you can take great comfort in the fact that there is not quite as much valid competition as you perhaps thought.

The other factor that might help to fill you with positive and empowering thoughts is this: although the great majority of aspiring theatricals, even the strongly talented ones, will face a long, hard struggle to convince one of the institutions of their choice that they are a right and proper candidate for training – having to face much scrutiny and perhaps one or more recalls – there are just a few who are so talented and wonder-fully gifted that it will be immediately appar-ent, and drama school will rush to offer them a place before another one does. Admittedly, these occasions are rare but they do happen and, therefore, it is not always the hopefuls who are competing for the drama schools – sometimes the drama schools are competing for the hopefuls.

Who knows – you might be one of these especially wondrous creatures, who are destined for great things and who, even at this early and preformed

Excellence in musical theatre training

Certainly for those wishing to pursue a career in straight acting, the accreditation system, as we have explored, is a reasonably sure and straightforward guide with which to make some fairly basic choices when investigating potential courses. For those wishing to take a musical theatre route, the system is of equal validity but slightly more complex and, if anything, offers a broader range of assured possibilities.

Many of those accredited drama schools offering acting courses also have good-quality musical theatre courses too. Some are better known for their musical credentials than others but, to all intents and purposes, you will find some fine potential and choice 'within the walls' of the National Conference of Drama Schools. In addition to this you will find other academies that are dedicated to the musical theatre world and whose courses exist more independently and apart from the culture of straight acting within the drama school environment. Again there are very many of these and there is perhaps even greater potential here for dubious quality within the content of the courses that they offer. However, as with drama schools there are some very fine examples too and it should not be difficult for you, with some research, to ascertain those with established reputations.

stage, are quite obviously such. It is unlikely, and not being so will certainly not mean that you will not succeed by a longer, more laborious route, but just knowing that such seeming reversals of power exist may serve as a talisman of hope and positive thinking to see you through the 'ordeal'.

SKIPPING AHEAD

We will return to what you can expect the life of a performing arts student to consist of and how being a drama student, of whatever kind, will change the way you look at the world of theatre, acting, performing and life in general, later in the book (assuming, of course, that you are successful in securing a place and are able to complete whatever course it is you undertake). For the time being, however, there are wider implications of auditioning that we need to consider. Therefore, let us jump ahead and assume for the moment that drama school has metaphorically chewed you up and spat you out or, in trepidation of this process, you have decided to undertake your career without pre-training. Now the whole process of auditioning exerts its relevance to your professional life yet again – only this time the prospects are much more serious as you begin the treacherous (but ultimately rewarding, we hope) search for work in the very hardest of all marketplaces!

OPPOSITE: **Musical Theatre Academies thrive and can provide an exciting mix of singing, dance and drama.**

3 Getting auditions: marketing yourself

THE NEED TO 'MARKET'

If you work as an actor in the professional theatre you are, in effect, running a small business. Admittedly, it is a business with only one employee and only one boss – you – but it is a small business nonetheless, and, as such, it must be run like one in every respect.

One of the most important aspects of running a small business (if not the most) is marketing the product or service that the business provides. In your case, that product or service is you and you must apply yourself diligently and effectively to the very important job of marketing yourself and promoting the quality of service you provide. It may seem very inartistic to view yourself in this way: after all, if you have made it thus far, you will no doubt be extremely talented, have invested much time, money and angst in your vocation and will have most likely spent considerable time and effort in vocational training at drama school or other establishment. However, if you are to succeed you must view your 'small business', at least in terms of its administration, in the same way a plumber, shopkeeper or any other kind of small business person does, and you must find your 'customers'

and persuade them to buy. It is certainly true that they will be buying 'you' in a most unique way – for it is your very self and the acting talent that you possess that they will be purchasing – but you are the commodity nonetheless and you need to be marketed and sold for the very unique product that you are.

One of the fundamental things to remember in this respect is that you are self-employed. It is true that sometimes in theatre jobs when working under an Equity contract you will be considered 'employed' for national insurance purposes (a situation that has caused much confusion to both actors and the Inland Revenue over the years) but essentially actors are freelance, self-employed people. Thus, in the same way that a plumber would find the most effective and successful way of obtaining and keeping clients who want to maintain the water systems of their homes, so must the actor work hard upon pursuing a very active marketing policy. Certainly, there may come a time in the plumber's career when he or she is so well known for the quality of their work that they can happily let the work flow in without much effort – and this can happen to a very select band of actors too – but until that time they must find and keep customers in a very proactive way.

Despite these observations, it is quite amazing how many actors do not work sufficiently hard at promoting themselves and obtaining work, despite being part of one of the hardest of all self-

OPPOSITE: **A talented performer must promote and market their talent in a variety of ways.**

employed professions. Indeed, if a plumber were to be as neglectful of this aspect of their working lives as many actors are, they would be out of business and finding an alternative career in a very short time. This being so, it is perplexing that actors can often exist within the 'business' for, sometimes, many years in the same woeful circumstances. So how do they survive as such?

The answer to this question is 'expectation': because an actor, from the moment they consider entering professional theatre in the first place, becomes saturated with the fact that theirs is a frighteningly dangerous choice of occupation and one in which they will constantly struggle and spend much time out of work. Because of this expectation an actor will not only adapt to this situation but will almost instinctively find ways to survive it: they will often find 'second string' jobs to maintain their livelihoods when not acting and they will adapt and compromise their lifestyles in order to remain actors in a way that a plumber never would. This is all good and proper and demonstrates the enormous levels of dedication and commitment that performers possess, but it can sometimes mean that the ability to survive without acting work leads, paradoxically, to an unnatural complacency in obtaining it. True, an actor will always emotionally crave the next job (sometimes to the point of obsession) but this very often fails to manifest itself in practical terms. At very best his or her efforts in this regard will stop short at sending out the odd letter and CV and scanning the 'job' pages of *The Stage* newspaper.

It is, of course, very unfair to label all actors in this way, and very many of them (especially those who are young and fresh from drama school) are boundlessly energetic in their approach to finding work. However, their efforts are often unfocused and lacking organized method and much time and money is wasted in useless endeavour. What these actors lack is a 'marketing strategy' – a phrase quite familiar to many other business people, but an anathema to many actors. However, there is absolutely no reason why this should be and it will help you enormously if instead of thinking purely in terms of 'getting auditions' you think more broadly about how you can market yourself as a talented and, almost more importantly, a 'useable' actor.

TARGETING

It is quite amazing how much time and money many performers put into sending out letters and CVs requesting auditions without targeting their efforts. Many theatrical employers will tell you that it is irritating and sometimes annoying to receive submissions that are not addressed to them specifically and which take no account of the actual or, at least, potential type of casing that may be available at that particular time. Applying for auditions in this way is wasteful of both time and money, and will offer a negligible success rate.

Most performers who canvas in this way do so by using various books containing lists of theatrical employers which they work through laboriously, sending out copious paper destined for the shredder. However, it is not these books that are at fault but the lack of method in their use. Therefore, having one of these books is wise; using them wisely is essential.

The very best of these publications, and the one that all performers seeking auditions should use, is *Contacts*, published by *Spotlight*. This is produced annually and contains comprehensive lists of theatre companies, theatres, agents, casting directors, drama schools, television and film companies, and theatre producers, both commercial and funded. Incidentally, it also includes most of the various organizations connected with the industry, and is thus a useful tool for actors generally, as well as for casting specifically. Each category

You must promote yourself relentlessly.

is divided into different types: for example, theatres are listed as *Alternative and Community*; *Children's, Young People's and TIE, English Speaking in Europe* (a more fertile area of employment than you may assume); *London; Outer London, Fringe and Venues; Provincial/Touring; Puppet Theatre Companies*; and *Repertory (Regional)*.

Target methodically and specifically

Your targeting should begin with an understanding of the various categories of production companies and the audition and, ultimately, employment potential (or perhaps more importantly, lack of potential) they offer to you specifically. Next you should draw up a list or highlight those which are relevant to you in terms of your age, experience and abilities as a performer. Then, most importantly, you should ascertain who it is in any particular organization you should write to. It is most important that you consider not just their job title but their actual name as well. Depending upon the type of company, the point of contact might be the artistic director, casting director or several other possible titles – many of which may be particular to the company concerned: the vital thing is to find out exactly 'who' they are and not just 'what', and then to contact them specifically and directly.

There are equivalent publications to Contacts in other countries too, or similar sources on the Internet.

PHONE AHEAD

If your copy of Contacts is up to date (as it should be – it is well worth buying each new annual addition as it is published) the contact information you need may well be accurately provided. If not, or if there is any doubt (remember that personnel can change frequently), it is well worth checking by ringing the company concerned. In fact, this is a wise and useful tactic anyway. Many performers worry that seemingly important people will be irritated by pestering phone calls. However, the reverse is often the case: many potential employers are impressed and sometimes flattered that a performer has taken the time and trouble to find out about them and their work. They are also much more likely to treat your eventual postal submission more favourably if they have already spoken to you, are expecting it and know that they have been carefully considered and targeted by you rather than being automatically mailed as just another 'name on your list'.

When making this initial contact you can also inquire about their work and possible casting opportunities that may be occurring at that time. You may well discover from this that sending your letter, CV and photograph is either immediately appropriate or best delayed until another time. Whatever the case, when you do write, remember to reference the conversation and remind them who you are. Provided this process is undertaken politely and respectfully, it is much more likely to result in consideration for an audition or at least your details being properly filed rather than heading for the bin. It will also allow you to make an equally polite and respectful call a sensible time after sending your information to complete the process. By working in this way you will have at least a chance or forming some kind of embryonic professional relationship with this

Don't be afraid to back-up your written submissions with a phone call.

contact which may yield fruit either now or in the future.

WHERE TO TARGET

A performer leaving drama school, or other forms of training, back in the 'good old days' may well have faced as daunting a task in finding work as today's 'troopers' do, but they were, at least, presented with a clear path to continue their ongoing experience and theatrical education. There was a time in this country when there was a strong local tradition of professional theatre in towns throughout the country and repertory theatres – presenting long seasons of plays, sometimes presenting different productions on a weekly or fortnightly basis – affording not only a reasonable amount of employment for performers and stage management but also allowing young people to learn their craft and extend their skills and abilities in a fast and furious manner.

Although repertory is not dead now, it has seriously declined and opportunities to work on a variety of productions in a concentrated period of time are limited to say the least. This deprives the performer of an essential ingredient of their progress: although training is essential (and in many cases thorough and of high quality), it cannot replace the 'on the job' training that is so necessary for the performer throughout their

Repertory theatre is a fertile learning ground.

career but especially in their early years within the profession.

Today repertory opportunities are severely limited and, although there are some notable repertory theatres still operating around the country, they tend, generally, to cast play by play rather than gathering a company of performers to cross-cast throughout a long season of different productions.

However, all is not lost for the graduating performer in today's climate. There are still some particular areas of employment to target, which not only offer the best opportunity of obtaining work for the fledgling, but also give some chance of a reasonable continuity of experience and learning. Two principal areas in this respect are commercial producers and 'Theatre in Education' – or TIE as it is generally known.

COMMERCIAL PRODUCERS

Commercial producers provide a comparatively rich area of possible employment for a performer and, especially for the new performer, should represent a major target in the quest for obtaining auditions and, ultimately, work. These are companies, often owned and fronted by one individual, which do not receive public funding (except sometimes in a 'backdoor' method), and are in the business of producing shows for profit: in essence they are businesses in the business of theatre. As such they often produce a reasonably large quantity of product and have a relatively high employment need and turnover of staff.

Much of a commercial theatre output is large 'number one' tours, playing big receiving houses (theatres that mainly take in touring products provided by independent managements) and often fronted by a recognizable actor from television to provide a draw to potential audiences.

This in itself is a good potential source of work but some commercial producers (often, though not exclusively, the smaller ones) also service venues with repertory seasons of commercially appealing shows (often thrillers, comedies and modest musicals) during times when they may not be inundated with other product. Sometimes the shorter of these seasons of plays will tour around, playing a series of plays at one theatre before moving on to repeat them (or some of them) at another. In a sense this is the surviving remnant of the repertory days of old and, as such, it is not only a good source of work but a desirable one too.

The most important thing to bear in mind when approaching a commercial producer for work is that they are business people and, as such, they desire to operate (and this includes casting) in as efficient a manner as possible – in terms of both cost and time. They often cast shows late or find themselves in the position where they need to recast – for whatever reason – quickly. Unlike funded companies, who may have at least some luxury of resources, they do not usually like to spend long periods of time holding auditions and will often cast people in the most convenient way. Because of this, your letter or phone call to a commercial producer has more chance of eliciting an immediate response than any other source of employment. However, in order to benefit from this you must target them positively and persistently. An explanation of this is best served by an example.

Don Oldman Productions (an entirely fictitious production company for our purposes) is rehearsing for a national tour of *When Did You Last Drop Your Trousers?* (an entirely fictitious play). During rehearsals the performer playing the 'funny vicar' part is struck down with meningitis and has to withdraw from the show. The production is due to open at a well-known regional theatre the following week. Your letter has just fallen on Don Oldman's desk (or you have just telephoned him) and you have played a vicar at drama school, or you mention in your letter that you know a performer

Be willing to ASM

Theatrical employers will often be more inclined to consider young or inexperienced actors if they are prepared to combine the role of acting with that of stage management. This is particularly true of commercial producers who are looking to make the most cost-effective and efficient use of their employment budget. For example, if a manager is casting a season of plays, a young actor may only be suitable for some of the plays to be produced. However, if they can also be utilized in a stage managerial capacity for shows in which they are not appearing as actors, then their employment for the whole season makes good and economic sense. Even in the case of casting one play, a commercial manger is more likely to give a chance to a new actor in a small part if they know that this actor will also be gainfully employed in other duties as well.

A performer who is also part of the stage management team is called an 'Acting ASM' (ASM standing for Assistant Stage Manager). It is strongly recommended that all young performers are prepared to undertake this role, not only in terms of making them potentially more employable, but also because of the invaluable training and experience opportunity that it affords them: nothing can provide the quality of grounding and breadth of experience quite so fully as working as an Acting ASM. For example, it is absolutely invaluable later in an actor's career to understand the demands and complexities of aspects such as lighting, sound, set, costumes, props, and to appreciate the difficulties involved undertaking these tasks. Also, having to get involved with the fundamental basics of theatrical production will help to keep the actor grounded and fully appreciative of all the roles undertaken by the team.

Therefore, when you are soliciting for work and auditions it will be of immense help to you if you make it known that you are willing to be an Acting ASM. Not only will this make you a more attractive employment proposition, it will help to establish that you have the right attitude about theatre – that you are prepared to learn and immerse yourself fully in the theatrical life. Whilst a career in the theatre can be immensely satisfying and enjoyable, it is not nearly as glamorous as many outsiders imagine – and your ability to demonstrate knowledge of this fact will be very advantageous.

If you do become an Acting ASM, make sure that you are a good one. Focus as much on the stage management as you do on the acting and don't get a reputation for shirking the 'nasty' jobs – you will command much more respect as an actor if you fulfil the whole role of Acting ASM with competency and enthusiasm.

You will find, however, that being a good Acting ASM can make producers reticent to employ you just as an actor. This, unfortunately, is an occupational hazard for many young and inexperienced actors and there does come a point in a performer's career when they have to politely decline work in order to move on. However, it is better to face this problem than having not started or established a career at all.

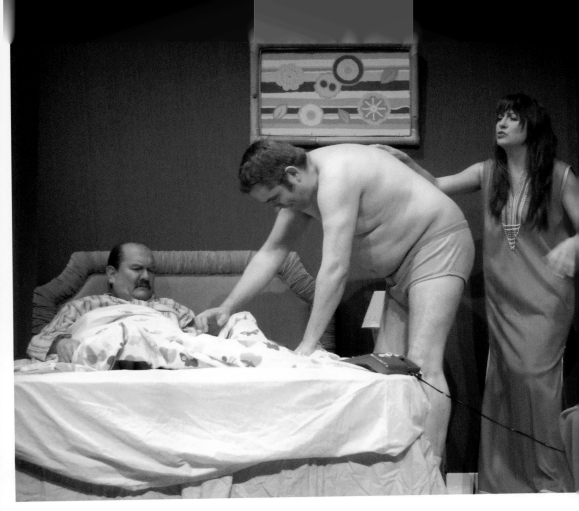

You must be proficient in a wide variety of genres and 'Farce' is a very specialist area.

who already works for him, or you are local to the rehearsal venue, or your persistence suddenly seems to him an indicator of commitment, or you give the impression from your submission that you are professional and hard working (thus good at learning a part quickly), and so on. Don asks you in for an audition and, rather than comparing you against many others, he is hoping against hope that you will read the part well and conduct yourself professionally, so that his problem is solved and he does not need to expend more time, money or worry in order to save his show before it has even opened.

Although this example may seem far-fetched, it really is not. However, benefiting from such a situation depends upon one very important factor. It is no use just sending out your letter, CV and photograph to every commercial producer in 'the book' and then sitting back to await developments. You must identify specific commercial producers whom you feel offer the kind of audition and work opportunities just discussed and then target them

Being a useful 'Acting ASM' will help to make you more employable.

politely but relentlessly: telephone them and introduce yourself and then follow up by letter or email;
look out for colleagues and friends who may have
worked for them before or, even better, currently;
take an interest in their work.

OPPOSITE: Theatre in Education is hard work but
rewarding, and an ideal place to start a career.

Getting an agent

Having an agent is something that most, if not all, performers aspire to. An agent can be invaluable in the process of obtaining auditions for theatre and is, to all intents and purposes, essential for television and film auditions. Therefore, if you are serious about a career as a professional performer you must turn your attention to obtaining representation as soon as possible. However, although you may need an agent, you need a good agent and an appropriate one for you and your circumstances – a bad or inappropriate agent is often worse than no agent at all.

So when you are approaching agents to represent you, it is essential that you do your homework. Make sure that you target agents who specialize in your field – particularly in terms of whether you are a musical theatre performer or an actor. Also, pick agencies that are about the right size for you: big enough to be successful and well known in the business but not so big and successful that you get 'swallowed up' and are not promoted properly by them. It can be particularly fruitless to be represented by an agent who has a large number of performers on their books of a similar age and 'type' to you, so try to find someone who needs you as much as you need them and who can genuinely see chances for you within their usual casting opportunities.

Having said this, a good and appropriate agent can be hard to get, as they will usually have a significant number of suitable people on their books already. One of the problems in obtaining an agent is the difficulty of convincing them of your merits and skills. It is for this reason that you must take every opportunity you can to invite your targeted agents to performances when you are working in the theatre. If you do not have an agent (or you have one but are looking to change) then you must see every theatre job as a means to showcase yourself to them (as well as other potential employers, of course).

However, it is notoriously difficult to get agents to attend performances, especially if they are not particularly looking for new performers anyway – so you must be persistent!

If you do obtain a good agent do not, whatever you do, rely upon them entirely. You must still pursue work yourself as arduously as before – an agent is a distinct advantage to you but not a substitute for your own marketing.

However, it is important that you are sensitive and reasonable in your persistence. Do not annoy them by constant bombardment but, rather, seek to instigate some sort of relationship with them in terms of keeping them in touch with your work and gently reminding them of your presence. You will often find that an initial introduction to these people may be afforded to you by a friend or colleague who knows or has previously worked for them. Therefore, the more working professionals you know (or, more importantly, know you) the better. Networking is obviously important in this respect and will be dealt with a little later in the following chapter.

THEATRE IN EDUCATION

This is probably the true successor to the old repertory system, not in terms of type of work (for it is obviously very different), but in terms of providing fledgling actors with the opportunity of high volumes of productions and performances in which they can hone and practise their craft. TIE companies tour schools and colleges providing entertainment to children and young people which is often (although not always) based in and around an educational theme. A typical production will often involve a small number of actors (usually with musical as well as acting skills) touring a portable set, costumes and props in a van to schools. In these cases all of the loading and unloading, setting up and stage managerial duties are undertaken by the performers and the company works very much as an ensemble unit. A typical day will include two performances at different schools and involves hard but rewarding work.

There has been a steady growth in this type of theatre over the years and TIE now provides one of the largest opportunities of theatrical employment for performers. When approaching a company for an audition it is vital that you advertise to them all of your relevant skills: no other form of employment will make use of skills such as juggling, tumbling, playing musical instruments, singing, physical comedy, and so on, to quite the same degree as TIE – being able to drive will also be a huge bonus.

Again, attitude is also very important here. These companies are looking for team players who will support each other and work hard to make the tour a success. They will also be looking to employ good communicators who will interact well with the staff at the schools and engage productively with the pupils. It cannot be stressed highly enough that these qualities are of vital importance in both this and all other forms of theatrical employment.

A number of TIE companies tour abroad in countries such as Italy, so it will be well worth your targeting these too.

Remember also that because most TIE productions will require acting, singing and dancing to a high standard, they are an equally good prospect for both those who are essentially musical theatre performers and actors who can also sing and dance to a least a respectable standard.

GETTING PRACTICAL

So now we need to examine exactly what needs to be done, and how it needs to be done, in order to make your self-marketing campaign a reality. So, prepare to work hard, market fiercely and read on.

4 Getting auditions: the practicalities

WRITING THE LETTER

When you submit your photograph and CV for consideration by a potential employer and request an audition, always write an accompanying letter. It is extremely annoying and, indeed, insulting to receive the pictures and CVs alone without any reference as to why they are being sent. A letter takes the trouble to introduce yourself and references why you are contacting this particular person in this particular organization. It allows you also to show that you have targeted that person and that potential job – rather than just casting your advertising material casually in all directions without really knowing or caring whom or what you are seeking out and why.

The letter should be friendly but concise and pertinent. It should tell the recipient why you have identified them as a person to contact and what you hope to achieve from the endeavour. Include any observations about yourself or your past work that are pertinent and relevant to this particular job or request for an audition. This applies even if this information is in your CV as well: you must draw attention to it and underline why it is of relevance. Do not make the letter too long and,

at all costs, avoid the temptation to make it funny, quirky or in any other way artificially outstanding: such tactics are irritating and do not serve their misguided purpose at all. That is to say, you might just capture the attention of one person in this way, who might like your style, but the many others you will alienate generally will more than negate the worth of this.

However, it is worth looking for an 'angle' for the letter, perhaps by referring to someone you know who has worked for this person or company (but ask them if you may do this first), or perhaps mentioning a show of theirs that you enjoy. Just be careful to use a light touch for this kind of approach and don't sound too ingratiating or, even worse, patronizing. In general, keep it short, to the point and, above all, professional!

As has already been established, this letter must be addressed to someone specifically. It must introduce you as a person and, most importantly, it must state why you are writing and what you hope to achieve in the process. If you are writing for a specific job, make it clear why you think you would be ideal for consideration. If it is a more general submission, give an idea of your knowledge of the company, or the specific director, and say why and how you feel that you would be able to make a contribution to the work that they do. Do not be afraid to be specific, although you should not sound arrogant; there is nothing to lose in being frank about your abilities, provided you feel confident that you will be able to back this up at an audition! Be enthusiastic and interested in their work. Of course, do not go over the top with this – you want to sound genuine – but if you are not genuinely excited by what they do you should not really be writing anyway.

It is always worth concluding the letter by saying that even if they have nothing to consider you for at present, you would be happy to visit them anyway, purely to introduce yourself for future reference. This is the performer's version of a sort of 'no obligations sales pitch' but provided it is kept casual it can produce a result in some cases – provided it is followed up.

THE ALL-IMPORTANT PHOTOGRAPH

Probably the most important tool in your marketing armoury is your publicity photographs or 'headshots', as they are often known. In today's world of on-line casting sites, directories and personal websites, performers can make use of a wide range of different pictures of themselves in both colour and black and white; in and out of character.

However, you will need one particular shot that is your main casting photograph for most general purposes. First and foremost, this must be a good-quality picture taken by an experienced and talented photographer. It should be in black and white (although may be taken in colour so that you can use this when appropriate) and can be taken indoors under lighting or outdoors, naturally lit. The latter of these two options often produces the best results but this is very much a matter of personal taste.

Choosing a photographer is no easy task as there are many to choose from. However, it is essential that you pick one who specializes in theatrical photography and is fully aware of the particular attributes needed of a good publicity headshot – a high-street photographer will not be appropriate, however good they may be. Obviously a personal recommendation is always a good place to start but you should make sure that you view the photographer's work to make sure that they have the right technique and take pictures that are appealing to you. A very good source is the aforementioned Contacts publication. This has not only a dedicated section for theatrical photographers but also has examples of their work throughout the book in the form of advertisements. This will

Writing a good letter is essential.

Following up: the phone call

Having sent your letter, together with a good photograph and CV, it will be tempting for you to feel virtuous in your endeavour and leave it at that. However, it is always worth following up your submissions with a phone call, inquiring whether it has been seen and gently expanding the request for an audition. So many performers shy away from doing this, often with the excuse that it will be intrusively irritating and do more harm than good. Undeniably, it can be a risky strategy, and might sometimes be counter-productive. However, remember that we are talking general tactics here and trying to play the best kind of game for success generally. You don't have a great deal to lose – it is unlikely that a phone call will irritate enough to make someone who had reacted positively to your letter and intended to offer you an audition change their mind out of spite. On the other hand, there is at least some probability that it will draw their attention to you and your merits – not least that of your commitment and temerity!

Therefore, in general it is a good practice but make sure that you are careful, respectful and easy going with it – do not be too intrusive and keep it all very casual and not intimidating in any way. Remember that theatrical employers are human too and may feel just as vulnerable to you as you do to them.

Do not follow up too soon: wait a while and then attempt to contact your targeted recipient to ask if they have received your letter and inclusions. You may find it difficult to get hold of them and do not be too persistent – after all, you are not a sales person – but a quick 'Hello' and a 'May I contact you again in the future?' is well worth attempting. Remember that although there are many actors writing, not nearly so many complete the task in this way, so you will be putting yourself at an advantage. Of course, as said, you risk annoying or irritating someone but, provided you are subtle, respectful and relaxed in your approach, this will not happen too often and, percentage wise, you will stand a much better chance of securing an audition or interview by using this targeted but comprehensive marketing strategy than just 'blanketing' employers with unsolicited and meaningless mail.

The important point here is that this is long-term marketing. If you get a good response from a contact, make a note of it and get in touch with them again after an appropriate interval. Nothing may happen instantly but in the long term the effort may start to pay off. Remember that if you do this consistently, eventually the sheer number of submissions should start to supply a reasonable number of ongoing audition opportunities – in the same way that for a sales person a certain number of leaflets delivered will obtain a certain number of appointments which will, in turn, secure a certain number of sales. This may seem very theoretical for an artistic person but being methodical in this way will give you the very best chance of success.

give you a very good idea of what to expect from each of them but, having pre-selected some possibilities in this way, you should then have a look at work on their website (or ask them to email you some examples) to examine a broad range of their shot-taking.

When you have your shortlist of potentials, contact them and ask for their charges. Although you will obviously want a good deal, avoid those that seem too cheap as there will probably be a good reason why they are! On the other hand, do not be afraid to ask for a discount if you are a new performer or a student: many photographers are willing to do this in order to secure business without making themselves look too cheap in their pricing generally.

A good publicity photograph should, of course, look attractive and appealing as a picture, but be wary of anything too glamorous or artificial. The most important thing is that it looks like you, as there is absolutely no point in obtaining an audition on the basis of an excellent picture, only to annoy and disappoint the director because your actual appearance is nothing like it. In addition to being an accurate likeness, the very best photographs of this kind are the ones that capture an essence of your personality or some element of your own personal style. It is for this reason that the best photographers in this field will take time to get to know you and relax you, before even starting to take pictures, and then engage you in conversation and 'banter' as they work, so that your pictures are natural and not in any way posed.

In the digital age it is really easy for photographers to take lots of shots, in order to give you a decent choice when selecting the ones you want to use. It is vital that they do this, as the first thirty or so will not be nearly as good as those taken when you have got used to the process and relaxed into a more natural 'you'.

When it comes to choosing your final selection (and especially that special one for general use), it will help you enormously to ask people who know you well to voice their opinion. Although the final decision must be yours, some outside advice will help you to choose a picture that does you justice and not just one that 'makes you look good' – a very different thing.

Although you will have the option of sending your photographs to managements electronically in their file format, it is usually better to send a proper hard copy print. Unless you have a very good printer at home, get these done professionally – there are companies specializing in reproductions for this purpose and the more you order the cheaper it will be. The best size to send generally is around postcard sort of size – although you will also need some 10 × 8 inch prints for displaying in theatre foyers.

Digital photography has also encouraged people to use friends to take their picture (or even take them themselves remotely). Although this can work, it is usually disastrous and it is much better to spend some of your advertising budget on a professional with experience and skill.

A final, and important, thought about photographs is this: change them regularly. People change quite quickly and constantly through life although, sometimes thankfully, we do not always notice this in ourselves. You should think about having a new set of pictures quite regularly (perhaps every two or three years) in order to ensure that they remain a faithful (rather than a flattering) likeness!

AN EFFECTIVE CV

The other mainstay of your advertising campaign, and weapon in your fight to secure auditions and work, is your curriculum vitae. This has probably the most potential for getting your marketing wrong in its compilation, so you must spend some time and thought getting it just right. The most important factors for its success are that it should be informative, accurate, concise and, above all, easy to read. If you have gained some experience it will be very tempting to detail everything you have done. Resist this temptation, or, if you feel that you must be complete for full justification of your career so far, do so in as clear and uncluttered a way as you can. Otherwise, be selective, and leave out things that will not necessarily impress, or duplicate another job of similar type and importance. If you are a new or inexperienced performer do not embroider or falsify your credits; do not hide your inexperience.

A CV needs to include two basic ingredients. Firstly it should give a potential employer basic information about yourself personally – not too much, but just enough to give a good 'snapshot' view of who you are and what your casting potential might be. Points to be included are:

- name;
- agent and their contact details (if applicable);
- contact details (as well as your agent's unless they prefer you not to do this);
- any websites or casting directories applicable;
- place of training and dates (this is most important and the first thing that most employers will look at);
- height;
- build (for instance, petite);
- hair colour;
- voice type and range (if you are a singer); and
- age and/or playing range. (Some people object to stating this, claiming that the photograph will give a reasonable idea. However, this can be most frustrating for directors, so include it unless you really prefer not to. If you include

Show reels, voice clips and casting workshops

These days it is vitally important for performers to have a show reel for television and film work that can be easily viewed by casting directors and other potential employers. The Internet and technology generally make the easy viewing part of this requirement straightforward. However, having suitable material, especially for those with little or no experience of filming, can be more of a problem.

There is a possible solution, and one that can also provide valuable experience and learning too, which is to get involved with low-budget and student films. You will find that a number of people and organizations are on the lookout for actors who are willing to work in their films for little or no payment – perhaps just expenses. In return they offer a free copy of the material that is filmed, which can then be used as a valuable source for show reels – there are specialist companies who will format and present this material for you in a professional way. As you continue to gain experience you can add and delete from your show reel as required.

Many of the Internet casting sites offer a special service that will enable you to offer yourself for opportunities of this kind. Always make sure that the people you are dealing with are legitimate and worthy.

Building up a library of usable voice clips is another valuable casting tool for radio and voiceover work. However, you should make sure that these are also presented professionally and are of high quality.

Another way of breaking into the inner circle of television and film casting is to attend a workshop held by a casting director. These enable casting directors to find and assess new talent, and can be a great way for you to start a professional relationship with them, which may eventually lead to castings and work.

your playing range be honest and do not push it too wide – it will not be taken seriously otherwise.)

Secondly you need to include your basic professional experience and skills. This should be detailed in the following sections:

- professional productions – detailed chronologically with dates, name of show, company and director (all clearly delineated in a structured format – some people prefer to reverse the chronology and this is fine provided it is clear what you did and when);
- accents – be honest and only list those that you are at least reasonably proficient in); and
- skills – again be honest but list everything that might be of use – for example, stage combat, dance skills, driving, riding, singing, instruments played (and to what level), juggling (but only if you are good at it as directors get bored with this inclusion), languages spoken, sports played (again, well) and anything else that might set you aside from the crowd, without fabricating or being ridiculous.

All of this is only a guide and you must compose and construct your CV in a way that makes you feel comfortable and honestly represented. However, you must make sure that it is set out clearly and accessibly. Keep it to just one page and format the page so that it is easy and quick to read – without any large sections of text or complicated detail. Everything should look smart, efficient and professional on the page. By and large, 'less is more' – so make sure you include all the important information but leave out anything that isn't strictly necessary.

Some CVs now include the performer's photograph at the top. With the advent of excellent home printers, this is a useful idea. However, it will not hurt to include an actual picture in the envelope as well, particularly if it is an important job that you are after.

In terms of professional credits, you may, of course, not have any yet. In this case it is perfectly acceptable to list your training credits (productions you appeared in during your 'finals'), provided you make it clear that this is the case.

NETWORKING (THE BEST OF ALL MARKETING TOOLS)

One of the disadvantages of being a performer is that you will often have to spend long periods out of work (or at least out of performing work). This can be turned to an advantage though, as it is the perfect opportunity for you to get out and about and meet people; do not sit at home waiting for the phone to ring. You must begin to develop contacts, not necessarily for any specific purpose but for the general broadening of casting opportunities.

Networking is one of the most reliable ways of getting work, although the word alone sends many performers into paroxysms of fear. This is strange as they are engaging in a profession where it can be ultimately essential, particularly as work in the theatre business gets harder and harder to obtain. It is simply the process of meeting and making yourself known (and recognized again) to as many people in the industry as possible. This is not by any means a short-term strategy; it is a cumulative process that may seem worthless for ages and then suddenly yield fruit. It is probably this 'slow burn' aspect of networking that makes it so unappealing to many people, yet as a long-term tool, underpinning your very existence as a performer, it is essential.

OPPOSITE: **An informative and readable CV is a must when seeking auditions.**

Ron Jesheth

Spotlight Page:????

Height: 6ft 1in

Hair: Light Brown

Eyes: Green

Weight: 13st

D.O.B. 23.08.58.

Training: Webber Douglas Academy of Dramatic Art

Contact: Tel: ????-???-???? or Mobile: ?????-??????

or email: ????@???.com

Previous Theatre

Thirty two years experience of extensive Repertory, No.1 Tours, London Theatres, Shakespeare, Children's Theatre and Pantomimes. Including:

Chesterfield Civic Theatre	Sergeant Match	What The Butler Saw
Chelmsford Civic Theatre	Gordon Whitehouse	Dangerous Corner
Westminster Theatre	Eeyore	Winnie The Pooh
Wimbledon Theatre	Reg	This Happy Bred
Theatre Royal, Nottingham	Remick	Suddenly At Home
Kings Theatre, Edinburgh	Elgin	Spiders Web
No.1 Tour	Mr. Beaver	The Lion The Witch And The Wardrobe
Charles Cryer Studio Theatre	Bertozzo	Accidental Death Of An Anarchist

Recent Theatre

National Tour	Pardoner	Canterbury Tales
Tabs Productions	Gerald	Woman In Mind by Alan Ayckbourn
Tabs Productions	John	Tomfoolery (Revue based on the songs of Tom Lehrer)
Stafford Gatehouse	Captain	Dick Whittington
Pomegranate, Chesterfield	Gilbert	Things We Do For Love by Alan Ayckbourn
National Tour	The Porter	Macbeth
Nottingham Theatre Royal	Inspector Cleaver	Murder With Love
Nottingham Theatre Royal	Bill Yorke	Sweet Revenge
Nottingham Theatre Royal	Inspector Hubbard	Dial M For Murder
Nottingham Theatre Royal	Nicholas Kendal	My Cousin Rachel
Nottingham Theatre Royal	Charles Stanton	Dangerous Corner
Nottingham Theatre Royal	Inspector Rough	Gaslight
Nottingham Theatre Royal	Richard Winthrop	The Ghost Train

Television, Video and Film

B.B.C. TV	Brooks	Thackeray - Omnibus (Dir: James Erskine)
Feature Film	Somerset	Mary Tudor
Shelley Masters Ltd.	Mr. Thrust	That's The Spirit
Partner Communications	Player	Golf
TV Choice	John Mentor	The Great IT Horror Story
TV Choice	Noble Father	Medieval Life

Skills: Folk Guitar, Ukulele, Driving, Juggling, Singing (light baritone), Drama Teacher (LLCM T.D.), Director-Producer-Writer.

Advertising yourself

All small businesses need to advertise and yours is no exception. Having obtained a good publicity photograph and collated relevant information about yourself, you will now need to look for places where you can display these. This will need to be done in quite the normal and unexciting way of paying various organizations to carry information and pictures of you to attract and encourage 'customers' to use your services.

There are many forms of this kind of advertising and one of your main concerns here will be deciding which of them to spend your money on. It may help to be very business-like about this and consider an annual budget which is within your means and allocate this amount to spend on advertising. You will then need to identify the best way of spending this budget in order to gain the best returns. Fortunately, the Internet has become a marvellous tool in the advertisement of performers.

Your first priority must be to submit your details to the main directory for performers, the aforementioned *Spotlight*. This directory is still the most widely used within the profession and, as well as being in book form, now allows employers to search and browse performers' details on-line. There are many other Internet casting sites too and many of them are worthy of your attention. The best way to research these is by recommendation and word of mouth, so ask around and discover which sites are producing a favourable number of auditions for people. Most of these, and certainly Spotlight, charge a fee for the service, so choose your submissions carefully and wisely. However, if you can only afford one it should be *Spotlight*, because (since the decline in power and strict entry criteria of the union Equity) membership of *Spotlight* is now often seen as the only true indicator of being a proper professional.

The huge advantage of *Spotlight* in particular, and of the other good online directories, is the ability they have to provide information about you in an easily 'searchable' format. For instance, if a director is looking for an actor who can speak fluent Cantonese, and you have this amongst your skills section, then when he types this into its search engine, your name and other details will appear – along with all the other actors who speak fluent Cantonese. Also, the online services allow you to display a number of different photographs, including some production shots of you in character if you wish.

Social networking sites, although not primarily designed for business use, have also become a prime place for performers to advertise what they are doing and network accordingly. Many performers now also have their own websites.

You should shape the whole of your working life (or your life when you are not working) around marketing yourself in this special way. The ways of doing it are endless and it is difficult to quantify the best ways to do it. In truth, it is the very doing of it that is important and not necessarily how it is done. You simply need to get out there and meet people.

One excellent way of proceeding is to go to classes and workshops frequently. This will have a double advantage: it will keep you tuned and help you to develop as a performer (essential in itself) and allow you to encounter directors and other industry people at the same time. However, don't become too obsessed with the importance of the people that you network with – a friend at your weekly dance class could easily be in a position to recommend you for a job at some point. Go to parties, socialize when you can, spend some time in the café of a theatre or television centre when you attend an audition, chat to people in audition waiting rooms, try to meet the director when you go to see a friend in a show, meet as many other performers as you can, keep in contact with colleagues and employers – these things, and many more, will help to raise your profile and keep you connected. Networking is a numbers game: keep playing it and eventually your number will come up.

An important word of warning: although your networking should be generally thorough and part of your everyday outlook upon your career, do not let it become too obvious or abrasive. Keep it effective but low key. There is nothing worse than a performer who makes their networking too overpowering and, thus, becomes marked out as being too pushy or invasive. Be sensitive to the task and do not let others see 'your wheels turning'. Think of the process as part of your overall philosophy and not as an obsession. In this way your networking will get you known and appreciated and not dreaded and to be avoided at all costs.

Finding auditions without an agent

If you do not have an agent then the whole process of finding auditions is up to you. As we have discovered, much of your work in this regard must be proactive and involve you in targeting various individuals and institutions and soliciting for work.

However, you must also be on the look-out for specific auditioning opportunities, where employers are seeking candidates for particular castings. Some directors will only use agents – perhaps having a trusted few that they regularly contact, and to provide good prospects for the parts that they are casting. But some will advertise auditions in other ways. There are various casting services that performers can buy into now – some postal but most online – and this gives the performer an opportunity to access what are often recent and genuine casting requests from a variety of employers. Many of these tend to be for the stage, as film and television casting directors still usually deal through agents only, but the spread of opportunities is broadening. Jobs are also advertised in The Stage newspaper (and other national equivalents) – although there is an obvious publication delay that comes into play here.

At the time of writing, Spotlight runs a service to its members whereby casting requests are emailed to subscribers who do not have agents – and many of these have provided auditions and jobs for those who have taken advantage of the service.

As with everything else, it is important that you research these various facilities and focus on the ones that are likely to provide you with the best results. There is no doubt that, generally, the Internet is revolutionizing casting for performers and, to some extent, beginning to break the 'stranglehold' agents have had in the past. You would be well advised to take full advantage of this as it continues to develop.

5 Choosing the right audition pieces

BE READY

It is something of a sad fact that, these days, auditions for professional jobs in the theatre industry do not tend to require the use of audition pieces; that is, it is rare that you will be asked to prepare dramatic or comic monologues for the purpose of demonstrating your talents and abilities. This aspect of auditioning is now almost entirely confined to entry into a drama school or other institution of training and it is not widely used in the profession itself. Therefore, if you are a prospective drama or musical theatre student this, and the chapters focusing upon training, will be of the most use to you. However, if you are beyond that stage there is still lots of relevance here, so read on.

Many (if not most) theatre auditions now require candidates to read from the script that is to be produced. This has always been done in the past, as it makes good sense to trial the person in the role, but whereas producers would often want to see prepared speeches as well, this now tends to be less of a priority for them. Television and film have broadly influenced this change, as they have always concentrated upon the script in particular, rather than a more general view of the performer's talents. One can see the reasoning here: the detail and intimacy of the screen will tolerate far less deviance from the performer's own persona and, therefore, it is necessary to focus upon the specific skills for that part. However, while the same is not true of theatre, the redundancy of audition pieces is now widespread.

This is a great shame and something of a false economy of time and effort on the part of producers. Yes, their main priority must, of course, be the particular play and part that is the subject of the audition, but it is also extremely helpful to glean a deeper and wider understanding of what the performer has to offer within their armoury of talents and skills. Watching a prepared speech or speeches will reveal this far more effectively than listening to someone reading a script unprepared. Sometimes those who give disappointing readings of the audition material will show themselves to be fine actors and performers when presenting their own speeches. Of course, the reverse can occur as well, and this is equally illuminating and potentially useful in avoiding mistakes when casting.

It is clear then that, once you have become a drama or musical student, and from thereon in, you will rarely be required (unlike your predecessors) to prepare audition speeches. However, this does not mean that you should abandon them – in fact they should still remain a focal point for your endeavours and a main aspect of your overall strategy for survival within the profession.

There are two basic reasons for this. Firstly, there

are still some theatrical employers who (despite the general trend) appreciate the advantage in seeing prepared work that has been chosen by the prospective employees rather than just relying upon cold readings of the script. This allows them to answer questions such as:

- How well prepared are they?
- Do they have good energy and dynamism?
- Do they make good decisions about themselves and the material they choose?
- Do they move well?
- Do they want this job enough to present themselves in a thoughtful and exciting way?

Therefore, because these insightful employers still exist (thankfully), it is a very good idea indeed to be prepared. Sometimes a producer will include this kind of request only to find that the surprised and unprepared candidate will have hastily and, therefore, sometimes shoddily prepared something that they perform in a less-than-satisfactory way – their nerves often exposing their lack of readiness. (Remember that there is often very little notice given when arranging auditions.) So, if you are prepared, you will not only find yourself at a tremendous advantage but also be able to maximize the opportunity of the audition to the full. Also, the more pieces that you have prepared, and the more varied they are, the better able you will be to tailor your offering to the particular job – earning you even more credit.

It may well be, of course, that you will be asked to prepare something specific or that, having done your research about the company and the job they are offering (as you should always do), you have nothing suitable in your repertoire and want to prepare something new anyway. In this case, the very fact that you are used to learning, rehearsing and maintaining a repertoire of prepared work will mean that you will be able to do this quickly and efficiently.

The second reason for having audition speeches as a fundamental part of your audition strategy is that there are benefits associated with choosing and developing them in the first place. As a working performer you should want to continue to improve and strengthen your skills by attending workshops and classes whenever possible; however, personal work (alone or with a tutor) is also vitally important to your development, and constantly rehearsing and expanding a range of monologues is an ideal way to keep your performing muscles in trim.

THE RIGHT PIECE FOR YOU

The first and most important criterion when selecting an audition speech is finding something that will suit you perfectly. It must suit you in not one but two ways: as a person and as a performer. It might be useful here to remember that these two are interlinked – in other words, however expert an actor you may be, your physical and psychological persona will inevitably structure, limit and enhance (in equal measure) the kind of parts and challenges that you will be able to undertake competently and effectively.

KNOW YOURSELF

It is vital that you do a little self-observation and analysis prior to building an auditioning repertoire, if you are to play to your strengths, and not be hindered by your weaknesses. You will need to think about the kind of person you are physically, mentally and (most importantly of all) emotionally, in order to find the best pieces to showcase your talents.

Although this aspect of audition preparation seems fairly obvious it is, for very human reasons, one that is often ignored. Many actors see themselves as a Mark Anthony or a Hamlet, many actresses as a Cleopatra or Ophelia (for instance), but not all of them will possess the qualities of strength, depth, appropriate age and emotional elasticity that these may respectively require. On the other hand, lack of self knowledge can often lead a performer to ignore a splendid part that others might be delighted, yet unable, to play – so having a good long look at yourself can often reveal some exciting possibilities for casting that might otherwise be ignored.

Always remember that if you expect others to cast you realistically and effectively, you must at least attempt to do this yourself too. This can often be easier said than done, however, as observing oneself honestly and dispassionately is not always straightforward. It will help you to enlist the help of others in the process: ask a range of your friends and colleagues how they see you as a person and the kind of parts they imagine you to be good for. Use their opinions collectively and generally (so that you do not become too fixated by individual comments) and only ask people whose judgement and honesty towards you is secure.

AGE

Always be realistic about selecting audition pieces that are the right age for you. For some, this will mean avoiding flattering yourself in choosing parts that you are now too old to play. For others, the opposite will apply: be careful to acknowledge your youth (if appropriate) and not select characters for which you are not yet old enough. Be realistic in this: for instance, Lady Macbeth is not old or even necessarily middle-aged by our standards, but neither is she in the first flush of youth. Anyway, even if she were, the depth of life experience of someone of her age when the part was originally written would be different to someone of her age now. In other words, a performer may need to be an older version of her than is factually appropriate in order to find the maturity and breadth of emotion needed.

PLAY TO YOUR STRENGTHS

Try to be honest and realistic about the kind of parts that you play well. You will probably want to develop a repertoire of pieces which broadly embraces both comedy and tragedy but, if you are selecting only one speech (or in choosing your principal selection), decide which of these two wide categories you are best at.

Think too about the emotional depth of any

Some modern (and not so modern) playwrights

You should become familiar with these for audition, and more general, purposes:

Edward Albee	David Henry Hwang	George Bernard Shaw
Samuel Beckett	Henrik Ibsen	Sam Shepard
Bertolt Brecht	George S. Kaufman	Stephen Sondheim
Anton Chekhov	Tony Kushner	Tom Stoppard
Caryl Churchill	Neil LaBute	August Strindberg
Noël Coward	Federico Garcia Lorca	Paula Vogel
Christopher Durang	David Mamet	Wendy Wasserstein
T.S. Eliot	Arthur Miller	Oscar Wilde
Brian Friel	Eugene O'Neill	Tennessee Williams
Maxim Gorky	Joe Orton	August Wilson
David Hare	Suzan-Lori Parks	Mary Zimmerman
Lillian Hellman	Harold Pinter	

potential piece and assess whether or not you are able, at this stage of your development as a performer, to rise fully to its challenges. If not, you would be better aiming for a less exacting selection but one that can perhaps showcase your acting techniques more generally rather than huge dramatic skills specifically. It is not necessarily a bad idea to choose a 'heavy' and emotionally deep scene for an audition piece, provided it is appropriate and that you are able to execute it properly and with the required emotional skill. If you cannot, then a less dramatically demanding selection may be a better bet.

Try also to find characters that are like you and reflect at least something of your own situation and life experience. It is obviously a great asset as a performer to be able to play a wide and diverse range of parts, but there is no particular advantage to be gained by stretching this ability unnecessarily in an audition. Pick parts that are comfortably within your grasp, range and ability, to ensure that you are able to apply your skills to maximum effect.

BE ORIGINAL AND INVENTIVE

A number of audition pieces are used again and again, and these 'old favourites' can become boring and uninspiring. Therefore, try to be as inventive as possible when you are selecting scenes to play. Yes, they need to be appropriate and to showcase the particular aspects needed at that particular audition but, beyond this, the more unusual and interesting as choices they are the better. A piece that has not been seen before (or,

You must know and understand yourself before you can become someone else.

at least, is not seen often) will capture the attention far more readily that one that is 'tried and tested'.

The best way to achieve this involves two basic strategies that are inextricably connected. Firstly, do not use audition scene compilation books too readily. Though these books can prove very useful and worthy shortcuts to finding pieces that you like and are good for you, they can also lead to the same selections being used again and again. Obviously, the most recently published tend to be the best, as they contain fresh ideas, often drawn from more recent plays. However, if they are good, their originality will be short-lived as more people come to use and rely on them. It is best to view them as a useful resource and reference, but not to rely on them in your decision-making.

Secondly, and as an alternative to this, make your selections from plays and works directly. In this way, although you will certainly cross-reference with the compilation books, you may also produce some original and inspirational choices that are not included in them at all. Most importantly, your selection and valuation process will be organic and individual and stem from your personal investigations rather than just pure recommendation.

This second strategy is not always easy, as you can sometimes struggle to know where to begin in your search for the right piece (this is why the books of ready-made selections can, despite their drawbacks, be a reasonable starting place). You will need to develop your own personal knowledge of dramatic literature as much as possible – especially, in this instance, new works. Fill as much of your spare time as possible with the reading of plays and visit the theatre as much as you can possibly afford. Always be on the lookout for new plays and new playwrights that may serve as potential sources for audition material.

INTERNET INFORMATION

There are many websites giving suggestions for audition speeches. Although there is potentially the same problem of repetition, the sheer depth of information and choice online will help to negate this and give you a much broader reference. Filter the suggestions carefully, though, and always give your own judgement the final say. After all, it is you who will have to face the audition panel, so make sure that you are comfortable with all your choices.

Past winners of the Royal Exchange Theatre's Bruntwood Prize for Playwriting

Research these, and as many other very new writers as you can, for audition source material:
Naylah Ahmed
Vivienne Franzmann
Matt Hartley
Ian Kershaw
Duncan Macmillan
Ben Musgrave
Fiona Peek
Phil Porter
Andrew Sheridan

BUILDING AN AUDITION REPERTOIRE

The ideal situation for the aspiring audition expert is to possess a repertoire of pieces that reflect not only a range of dramatic genres but also a range of potential within themselves. The basic requirement is to have a few pieces of differing types and styles, although this can be extended in time and a performer's repertoire will not suffer from becoming extensive.

In fact, although it may seem excessive in light of the unfashionable nature of this approach to auditioning to have a large number of audition speeches, it can sometimes prove a distinct advantage. Once, an actor was invited to attend an audition held by a commercial producer for a part in a planned tour of quite a famous thriller. The actor was asked to perform the two contrasting speeches that had been specified via his agent and was then expecting to leave only to await the hoped for call to employment. To his surprise he was asked if he possessed yet another prepared piece, then another and then another. Fortunately, having recently graduated from drama school, this particular actor was able to oblige (although he had to delve very deep into his memory by the end). It transpired that, as well as planning the tour, the management concerned was also considering a long weekly repertory season in which a string of very contrasting plays was to be produced. This actor, although having been called for the tour, appeared on the day highly suitable for the season instead, and the management wished to see how well he could cope with a wide variety of styles and content. The moral of this story is not only that to be armed with many audition pieces could one day be a distinct advantage, but that one can never tell what opportunities an audition, or indeed any contact with a theatrical employer, may bring – and, thus, preparedness is of vital importance.

With this in mind it will now help you to consider the basic styles and types of piece that should be the foundation of your stable of auditioning material.

Firstly you should have a piece of Shakespeare or, if possible, two – one comedy and one tragedy or history play. Supporting these should be two modern pieces, one comedy and one straight – preferably quite (but not too) dramatic and emotional. These should be seen as the very basic requirement. In addition to these, the repertoire would be complemented by the addition of a nineteenth-century piece – perhaps Chekhov and a Restoration comedy scene. Other useful possibilities for further depth could be a George Bernard Shaw, an Oscar Wilde, a Noël Coward and, best of all, a larger selection of contemporary speeches containing a variety of comic and dramatic intensity.

The older playwrights

Develop your understanding of these playwrights, in order to extend your audition repertoire still further. Alternatives to Shakespeare can be exciting:

George Farquhar
John Fletcher and Francis Beaumont
John Ford
Ben Jonson
Thomas Kyd
Christopher Marlowe
Thomas Middleton
Molière
John Webster
William Wycherley

CHOOSING AN AUDITION SONG

Selecting songs for auditions is not only the preserve of the musical theatre exponent. Actors may be required to sing at certain auditions too, especially if the casting is for a pantomime or a season of plays that may contain a musical or a play with songs (which is not the same thing).

In general this should be a song designed to show off a wide range in the performer, both in terms of pitch and musical ability – without being too ambitious if for the use of an actor rather than a musical theatre performer. It should, in most instances, be from a recognized musical but not, if possible, one that has been produced too extensively or is so old that it appears hackneyed and obvious. A song with a story or dramatic interest is best and one that builds to some sort of a climax or intensity is also desirable.

If it is possible to have more than one song to perform, then a reasonably up-tempo number and a ballad would make an ideal pair. If you have only one song – some actors may feel this is sufficient – then the choice between ballad and up-tempo really depends upon personal preference and your type of performance personality. However, if possible it is better to have at least two – even for the less musical actor!

A ONE-PERSON SHOW

By now you will have realized that the intention of this chapter is not just to equip you with some potential audition speeches, but to use the exer-

Don't forget the Greeks and Romans (we owe it all to them)!

Aristophanes
Euripides
Plautus
Seneca
Sophocles
Terence

cise as a means of establishing and developing an ongoing professional development that is palpable, observable and quantifiable. A good way to structure your work is to develop your pieces around a theme, thereby giving you the basis of a one-person show – should you ever find yourself in need of one!

6 Preparing for the audition

AN OVERALL ATTITUDE

Before considering how you should prepare mentally, emotionally and practically for specific auditions and their particular requirements, it will be valuable to think a little about your attitude to auditions generally. Auditioning is one of the most important (and therefore most potentially stressful) elements of your career as a performer and, in order to have a dynamically positive view of the process without letting it dominate your life and wellbeing, you will need to make sure that you have a sorted and balanced outlook upon it from the start.

A good and simple way of achieving this is to use a line from the great poet T.S. Eliot: 'Teach us to care and not to care'.

TEACH US TO CARE …

You will and, indeed, must care deeply about auditions (and, more specifically, their outcomes), for it is these that instigate, propagate and develop your career as a performer. The job that you have chosen is unique in the sense that you are constantly having to resubmit yourself for work via an interview process (which is what an audition essentially is), and this focuses importance

OPPOSITE: **Dress appropriately for the part you are auditioning for, but do not go too far!**

upon auditioning in a very strong and persistent way. It is therefore vital that you approach every single audition that you attend with an extremely positive and energetic frame of mind. Even in the rare event of attending an audition for a job that you don't really want, the people you are auditioning for may well be casting other projects, and every new meeting with an employer is a potential professional relationship for the future.

Sometimes it is difficult to find a positive mental approach to an audition: you may be tired, dispirited, under the weather, or have your mind upon other issues in your life. But you must try conquering these feelings and present yourself in the best possible way.

The best way to find a positive mental attitude is by focusing upon the product you are selling – you! It is all too easy to approach a casting in an apologetic way: doubtful of your own abilities and nervous of yet more rejection. After all, rejection is part and parcel of a performer's career and it can have a cancerous effect upon your confidence. Therefore, you must think about the audition not just as a test which you may or may not pass but as an opportunity for you to present your talents and abilities to people who may very well want to take advantage of them. Remember, too, that an audition is not one sided – you are finding out about the job and the employer at the same time as they are finding out about you; in a sense, you are interviewing them as well as they you. You must have faith in yourself as a performer (for otherwise

'Teach us to care and not to care' is a very worthwhile mantra, courtesy of T.S. Eliot.

there is no point in you pursuing the career at all) and you must make every attempt confidently (as opposed to arrogantly) to convince the audition panel of your worthiness.

... AND NOT TO CARE

Having undertaken an audition and given it the best and most productive effort you possess, you must then forget about it. So many performers waste much of their time and precious emotions waiting for a result after an audition, only to be disappointed eventually or hear nothing else about it at all. You should think of every audition you do as a very important part of your professional duties that will, cumulatively, lead to various forms of employment but as individual events may not. Remember that if you do not get the part you have not necessarily failed: it may be that you were the wrong height, not quite as suitable for the role as someone else, or simply not quite the right age. Casting is a very complex process and its execution can take many a twist and turn of which the performer is only rarely aware. Therefore, give the audition your very best shot and then move on to

the next one: it will be delightful if the telephone rings telling you that you have the part, but if it doesn't then that is part of the job and by then you will be focusing upon another opportunity anyway. Although it is easier said than done, try not to become emotionally dependent upon the result of any one particular audition – you will have a much happier and, ultimately, more productive career.

It may be useful to look at the casting process in much the same way as a direct salesperson may look upon selling. First they have some leaflets printed (making sure that they are attractive and describe the product accurately and attractively). A hundred leaflets may produce three sales presentations (in which they do their very best to sell the merits and advantages of buying the product). From those three presentations will, on average, come one sale – the commission from which will provide recompense for the time and investment spent on the whole process. Although this is rather a cold and calculating example, and perhaps one not that empathic with an artistic process, it may help you to view auditioning as a general means

What to wear

The first and most practical decision to be made about any particular audition is how to present yourself physically on the day. Choice of clothing is very important and, in making your decision, you should focus very much upon the part for which you are auditioning.

However, while it is necessary to be dressed appropriately for the role, it is not necessary to 'go in costume'. For instance, if you are attending a casting for an army officer who is facing a court marshal it might be sensible to wear a suit in order to find the feel of the appropriate uniform, but it is not necessary to hire a uniform complete with swagger stick. The former of this rather extreme example will enable the panel to view you in the correct way; the latter will simply subject you to ridicule once you have left the room.

If there is no identifiable form of dress for the part, or (more likely) you do not know exactly (or even vaguely) what the part is beforehand anyway, then you should wear clothes in which you feel comfortable, and which you feel honestly reflect your own personal sense of style. It is important that you look as if you care about the encounter and your appearance, but it is equally vital that you feel at ease and as relaxed as possible. Many male performers, for example, will wear a jacket to an audition as it provides ample pockets in which to place hands. However, be careful, as this is not advisable if physicality is particularly important within the role and the panel may want to see your unencumbered physical shape.

Remember that directors may be seeing lots of people – make sure that you are memorable in appearance, but for the right reasons. Dress and appearance can really help to illustrate how right you may be for a part in the mind of a confused and beleaguered director trying desperately to remember and evaluate all the people she or he has seen that day – or even week!

It may seem obvious, but do make sure that you attend auditions in a clean and reasonably well-groomed state: just because they work in the arts does not mean that members of an audition panel are not adversely affected by poor personal hygiene and scruffiness.

to an end within a career structure, rather than a series of individual trials and obstacles to be overcome.

DO YOUR HOMEWORK

Before we look further into the audition itself and the preparation that may be required, there is one piece of general homework to draw your attention to. It is to make sure that you attend with some knowledge of the company that you are auditioning for, the director in charge of the particular production in question and, if possible, the project itself. This will not be necessary if you have applied for the job because you are already interested in and admire the company and director, but it will not be uncommon for you to obtain the casting, perhaps via an agent, without any pre-knowledge at all. In this case, and provided you have enough notice to do so, make some enquiries and do a little research so that you have at least a basic idea of what and whom you will be encountering. This will allow you not only to engage in the audition with confidence but also demonstrate that you have taken an interest and concern in the job. Provided that you do not make this look to obviously like sycophancy it cannot but help you in your cause and will be a worthwhile investment of time. The Internet is an obvious tool for this type of investigation, but asking around your friends and colleagues will usually unearth some information too.

WARM UP

Most professionals would not think of starting a performance without in some way warming up their body, voice and, sometimes, their 'acting muscles' also. However, there are many who do not seem to think this is as important for auditions. On the contrary: it is of vital importance and many a poor or lacklustre casting has resulted from a participant technique being cold and clunky – particularly if it is early morning. So you must put a strategy in place that will make sure that you are focused and ready in both body and mind. The mind part here is of equal importance and your acting technique will need just as much warming as your vocal and physical – perhaps more so. Everyone has different ways of warming up and the exact nature of the process is not all that important – just the doing of it. However, to give you an idea of a possible warm-up that might suit your needs on such an occasion, we will look at a very basic suggestion of one.

Ideally, you will be able to do this on site – even if you have to disappear into a lavatory to do so. However, with the best will in the world this might not be possible in practice. So it is suggested that you do it before you leave the house and then repeat it at the venue if you have a chance. Don't forget to leave enough time for this and remem-

ber, not having to rush and panic will help your general attitude and demeanour.

AN AUDITION WARM-UP

There are three basic elements to this warm-up: body, voice and mind. It can be done at the audition venue if facilities and time allow (it is especially designed not to make too much noise), but can be expanded for home use.

1. Stretch your arms and legs in all directions – up down and to the side. As you do this take a nice deep yawn to open up your throat. This should feel like arising in the morning – just getting everything woken up. Extend the stretch right down into your fingers and toes.
2. Gently roll your shoulders forward and back in circular motions. Do this gently and carefully, it is simply to ease out any tension, not to stretch or over-exercise the muscles too much.
3. Let your head drop slowly down so that your chin touches your chest. Hold this for a second and let the weight of your head perform a natural and gentle stretch upon the neck muscles. Now slowly rotate the head over one shoulder, going back to upright and then continuing round and down again over the other shoulder. Continue this circling motion a few times and then change direction. (Note that the head should drop forward in the rotation but not back, as this might cause strain or injury.)
4. Shake each limb in turn, starting gently and then becoming a little more vigorous. Make sure that the shake includes the hands and feet.
5. Put your feet shoulder-width apart with your feet pointed slightly outwards, tuck your posterior under and imagine that you are being suspended from the ceiling by a piece of string attached to the crown of your head. Enjoy this feeling of elongation and standing

up straight, and try to relax all of the muscles that are not involved in the process.

6. As you stand in this way start to 'chew' around with your jaw and involve as many of the face muscles as possible so that you are gently stretching and agitating all of your face – this should have the effect of looking like you are 'pulling faces'.

7. Next, take a long, slow, deep breath in through your nose – trying to feel it going deep down inside yourself. As you do so keep your shoulders down and relaxed. Hold the breath for a count of three seconds and then slowly exhale until you are quite empty. Hold this empty state for another count of three seconds and then relax and allow your body to fill up again quite naturally and fully. Repeat this six times but do not make yourself feel giddy in the process.

8. With another long deep breath exhale on an 's' sound (like escaping gas) and keep this very steady, trying not to waver or splutter – it should be a constant, smooth sound and be fully under the control of your breathing muscles so that the air escapes as one long, fluid 'line' of sound.

9. Repeat this but with a gently hum upon any comfortable note – remaining equally steady and under control throughout the outward breath. This does not need to be too loud but should be gently pushed forward into the face, so that you can feel your lips buzz. Do this three times.

10. Put your hands onto your face and gently stroke downwards each side so that your jaw is pulled down and your mouth opens wide. Let the jaw relax completely as you do this so that your mouth hangs open wide – but quite naturally, without forcing.

11. Repeat step nine but, after you have established the hum each time, let the jaw drop open and continue the outward breath on an 'Ah' sound (as in the word 'car'). Again, this does not need to be loud (if you are at the venue in the lavatory say) but it should remain smooth throughout the breath and the jaw should be fully relaxed – completely dropped and mouth open.

12. Next speak a tongue twister such as this, in order to wake-up your articulation:

Mary and Peter popped down to the pickling parlour with many a dazzling diva dangling down in a theoretically theatrical pose and wearing a mink, monogrammed and quite majestic but thoroughly cute, kind and contentious cotton milking mock-up of a silk Sagittarian's sock sorter – steamed in the very same sort of surreptitious way that Suzy Sherman used to stitch her voluptuous stockings when she sheltered in the very same vending vehicle tyre tracer that Tom Tinker used to use at the Vatican's loose and languid luscious lingerie lock-ins at the local fishfinger foundation factory in 'Many Merry Mace Hartington on the Wallop' – which is a wilderness where many merry mangling miners meet to discuss nearly ninety-nine newly minted needle knitters needed for Barry Bradshaw's terribly tedious but tight and terrifically tenuous shelter shredder shape shifting pool parties.

Start this slowly and build up the speed through three repetitions – if there is time. Do not try to attempt this in one breath – just snatch an intake when you need to.

13. Now speak this line out loud – clearly, slowly and without particular expression: 'Can you tell me what this is please?' Now repeat it, but with expression suited to each of the following situations:

Warming-up is vitally important when auditioning.

- You are in a shop and are pointing towards an item on a shelf.
- You have just found a cigarette butt in your teenage child's bedroom.
- You are showing your doctor a worrying lump on your arm.
- You are about to reveal a surprise and exciting item from beneath a cloth.
- You are pointing to a disappointing mistake in your student's exercise book.
- You have just found a gun in your partner's bag.
- You are embarrassingly uncertain of an French word on a menu.

14. And now the same with this line – 'I think that depends on you and how you feel about it!' – and in answer to the following different imaginary questions:

- Shall we go to that party tonight?
- Do you think that I ought to take the job or not?
- Our relationship is over, isn't it?
- Shall I wear this top?
- Do you think I will ever be able to give up smoking?
- Now that I have this gun pointed at your head, what do you think is going to happen?

15. Speak this short extract from Shakespeare's *Henry V*. It is a chorus speech and should be spoken with enthusiasm, energy and colour.

    O For a Muse of fire, that would ascend
    The brightest heaven of invention,
    A kingdom for a stage, princes to act
    And monarchs to behold the swelling scene!
    Then should the warlike Harry, like himself,
    Assume the port of Mars; and at his heels,
    Leash'd in like hounds, should famine, sword and fire
    Crouch for employment.

16. Finish by running through one of your audition speeches – even if you are not expecting it to be required for the audition. If you are expecting to be performing speeches and you have been asked for two or more, then do them all. You are now ready to do battle!

Singing and dancing

Unlike acting, it is virtually impossible to sing or dance effectively (or safely) at all without warming up. Therefore, if you are required to sing or dance at an audition you will, most likely, have your own means of warming up for these, extended from your training and ongoing classes and instruction. However, although those performers whose background and training lie within musical theatre will ensure that they are adequately warmed up vocally and physically almost by instinct, actors may not – so whatever branch of theatre you come from, make sure that your preparatory work is thorough and effective.

7 Working on audition pieces

In this chapter we will look at how to prepare and rehearse monologues for audition. You may of course be working with a teacher, in which case you will be placing much of the responsibility for your development into their hands. However, for the sake of simplicity here, we will assume that you are working alone.

The early part of the chapter will deal with some basic and general acting and performance techniques applicable to audition speeches, and later rehearsing specific types of speeches will be looked at. For both aspects, a series of exercises is included and these should not only be read but practised too. It must be assumed that you have the talent, but successful auditioning, like all aspects of the world you are entering, is about craft also – your ability to apply your talent – and the development of craft requires regular, and often painstaking, practice.

If you are having regular lessons then discussions with your teacher should establish your time-frame and timetable for your work alone. If not then you will need to instigate this yourself. Do not be vague about this; set aside certain available timeslots within your week so that you are able to stick to a regular and disciplined routine.

ACTING TECHNIQUE

This is obviously a very wide subject and it would be impossible to do it justice within a single chapter, but let us engage with a few basic ideas and concepts for now, in order for you to be able to prepare monologues. Remember that their purpose in this context is not to perfect displays of acting and performing but to showcase potential, and it is to this end that our efforts need to be directed.

BEING SPONTANEOUS

There are very many aspects to good acting but the most important (simply because it underpins all of the others) is spontaneity. This is the ability to make text seem as though it is not written down at all, but springing from the mind of the character in 'real time'. This allows you to be real, truthful and natural in a way that defies the artificiality of the situation. It brings the written word to life and gives meaning to both character and situation. A useful way of contemplating spontaneity is this: playwrights turn life upside down – they dictate words and actions before thought. Performers need to turn this back upright again by providing the thoughts that inspire the words and actions. Therefore questions like, 'Why am I saying this?' are far more important than, 'How shall I say this?' The first of these questions may lead to spontaneity and reality; the second to mere demonstration and artificiality.

If we analyse spontaneity we will see that it contains a plethora of elements such as pace, pausing, modulation and emphasis. However, to analyse something is often the very way to lose it, and this is the case with spontaneity. You will certainly need to know what it contains and how to achieve excellence in its various elements, but to practise it consistently you will also need to address it at its root – 'the thought' – and, to a certain extent, trust the natural communication abilities that you possess as a human being to do the rest naturally. In other words, you cannot feign spontaneity, you have to be spontaneous – but against the artificial backdrop of knowing what you are going to say and do in advance (not to mention having lots of strangers watching you intently while you do it!).

Much of spontaneity is achieved with other actors. By its very nature it is based upon reaction and interaction: upon listening, thinking and then speaking (or doing). However, keeping to the premise that you are working alone, we will focus upon exercises that can be practised as such.

EXERCISE 1: SPONTANEITY A (ADDING THOUGHTS)

1.   Read through the following piece of text and become completely familiar with it:

It's cold today. That's why I'm so well wrapped up. But it's warm in here. Do you mind if I take my coat off? It's always so snug in here. It feels comfortable. Always. How lucky you are to live here. How's Harry?

Note that this little speech is, to some extent, deliberately poorly written and awkward – in order to make it more of a spontaneity challenge (the very best writing always lends itself to spontaneity more readily).

2.   Decide for yourself exactly what the situation is – who you are, where you are, who you are visiting and why and, most importantly, who is 'Harry' and how important is he to the encounter. When working upon real plays many (if not all) of the answers to such questions would be obviously apparent within the plot. However, there may still be scope for your own imagination and interpretation and for this exercise you need to invent a complete scenario in your mind to match the text.

3.   Write out the speech on a piece of paper and add, in brackets, what your thoughts are before each sentence. Thoughts do not always match words in an obvious way, so while your thoughts for the first sentence – 'It's cold today' – might contain 'I'm feeling cold', they might just as well contain 'I'm embarrassed and need to say something to break the silence'. Of course this will depend to some extent upon the situation you have devised, so make sure your decisions reflect and accord with that.

4.   Now perform the speech (having committed it to memory first), using the bracketed thoughts to motivate not only your speaking but your movement too. Try doing it several times and allow it to be different each time. Do not predetermine what will happen – just use the thoughts you have written and 'go with the flow' each time. You will be surprised how much life and spontaneity the scene will take on and how much variety you will achieve in each repetition of it. Do not 'nail anything down' – if something works one time, don't necessarily try and make it happen again; your acting should have a life of its own. The process should feel risky but exhilarating.

5.   Finally, continue playing the scene but now, if inspiration takes you, change the thoughts as you go along. Make sure that you stick to your scenario as devised but allow each motivating

thought to develop or morph completely if it wants to. Do not force anything, but be sure that you keep thinking – so that each word and action is preceded by free, liberated but appropriate, thought.

SPONTANEITY THROUGH PACE

Pace is very important for the actor, both in terms of finding the correct pace, and in variety of pace. Pace is not the same as speed in general – how fast you go – as this, in itself, is not nearly so important. Pace is about how quickly you 'pick up' the dialogue after the preceding speech, what pauses you do or do not leave, and how quickly or slowly you react to stimulus. Correct pace is vital in order to progress a play or scene without it flagging or becoming too weighty and boring. However, it also has a very specific application to spontaneity. The reason for this is that control of pace is directly related to thought and, in particular, speed of thought: it is how quickly or slowly a character thinks (and how this changes) that allows the actor to control pace naturally and without artifice. Speed of thought is vital in terms of spontaneity because it gives your performance variety and life.

If you look and listen to someone in 'real life' you will notice all the various subtle changes of voice and movement that they make as they go about the business of living and communicating. You will see lots of little inconsistencies, quick alterations of emphasis, odd movements, sudden changes of focus, slowing and quickening of delivery, jumps in tonal register, facial ticks – the list goes on. All of these things make them appear spontaneous (this is not difficult for them as they are living their life forwards and not in a strange retrospect as an actor has to operate in a play), and the spontaneity arises not just from thought but the speed of thought: as the brain process all the various stimuli, contemplates things, and assesses and evaluates, so it feeds the voice with naturally paced thoughts of different intensities and speeds.

All of this happens naturally – in fact it would be impossible for it not to happen. However, you would be surprised how easy it is for an actor to 'flatten out' all of this and to think at a constant and unvaried pace – as if the constancy of appearance of the words on the page somehow needed to be recreated in their delivery off the page. It is this mistake that contributes most to actors appearing unnatural, artificial and wooden. The good actor must not be word-centred but thought-centred, and if you can change and vary your speed of thinking you will have found a very reliable shortcut to spontaneous acting.

Aligned and connected to this is a technique known as 'New Thought Energy Injection'. This is when a new idea will suddenly occur to a character and interrupt their flow at a new speed. Such an injection of spontaneity can be quick or manifest itself as a slow realization, but it always has the effect of re-energizing the dialogue and making it natural.

EXERCISE 2: SPONTANEITY B (SPEED OF THOUGHT)

1. Read through this next piece of text and become completely familiar with it:

I went to see Peter today. He's still living with that awful woman – I really don't know what he sees in her. Did you know that she used to be in the army by the way? Not surprising really – she orders him about as if she was a sergeant major! I wonder if that's why she's so meticulous about everything and tidy – I hadn't thought of that. Anyway, what did I want to tell you about Peter? Oh yes, he's managed to have a look at that stuff you sent round and he thinks – only thinks, mind you – that some of it might be quite valuable! He's going to take it into that shop he told us about and get the guy in there to have a look at it. I don't think it's anything to get excited about but you never know! Although, Peter's pretty honest – if it was a pile of old junk I think he would have told us. He's a nice bloke Peter – I feel very sorry for him really – especially now after all that business with the boiler last week. By the way have you seen my best pen? I put it down in here yesterday – at least I think I did. Anyway, I told him to let us know. He's looking very thin you know – I don't think she feeds him properly!

2. Try speaking it aloud a few times to get used to it and then rehearse it using this version which has thought speeds and new thought indicators suggested in brackets just before the words they refer to. Attempt to apply these and see if you can make them work to give the scene shape and a natural feel. You should be aiming to align the changes of pace to a natural and spontaneous thought process that harnesses attitude and feeling as well. Remember that you should be changing the speed of the thought and not just the speed at which you say the words.

I went to see Peter today. (**Quick new thought**) He's still living with that awful woman – I really don't know what he sees in her. (**Slowing**) Did you know that she used to be in the army by the way? (**Quicker**) Not surprising really – she orders him about as if she was a sergeant major! (**Slow new thought**) I wonder if that's why she's so meticulous about everything and tidy – I hadn't thought of that. (**Very quick change to fast**) Anyway, what did I want to tell you about Peter? (**New thought but at same pace**) Oh yes, (**Back to original pace**) he's managed to have a look at that stuff you sent round and he thinks (**slightly quicker**)

only thinks, mind you – that some of it might be quite valuable! (**Gentle new thought**) He's going to take it into that shop he told us about and get the guy in there to have a look at it. (**Gentle new thought**) I don't think it's anything to get excited about but you never know! Although, Peter's pretty honest – if it was a pile of old junk I think he would have told us. (**Slower**) He's a nice bloke Peter – I feel very sorry for him really – especially now after all that business with the boiler last week. (**Very quick change to fast**) – By the way have you seen my best pen? (**Slowing**) I put it down in here yesterday (**Very slow**) – at least I think I did. (**New thought to medium pace**) Anyway, I told him to let us know. (**New thought slightly faster**) He's looking very thin you know – I don't think she feeds him properly!

CHARACTER BUILDING

A fast and fundamental examination of acting techniques would not, of course, be worth consideration without mention of characterization and, in particular, character building. One of the great joys of acting is simply being someone else – the inhabiting of another person and the discovery of their world.

In studying character, albeit briefly, it is important to be realistic. You are not really able to create another being out of thin air. All of your characterizations will be extensions (perhaps even exaggerations in some cases) of yourself. You have only yourself to work with – your brain to think the character's thoughts and your voice and body to give them life. Therefore, you should always think of characterization as starting with 'you' and developing onwards and upwards into another persona. In this way you will use your own resources naturally and truthfully, and your characters will have real life and be credible.

In life we think at different speeds, and doing this when you are acting will bring further spontaneity, reality and truth.

This is not to say that characterization necessarily has to be subtle in order to be truthful. Although you will often play characters close to yourself, sometimes they will be quite outrageously different and their foundation will be large and expansive. Indeed, it is important for a first step into character building that you experiment with the 'larger' side of the process. In order to do this you could spend some time with children's theatre – a rich potential of employment in itself, a source of possible auditions and a genre that you will almost certainly come into contact with many times in your professional career.

EXERCISE 3: CHARACTERIZATION A (LARGE AND LOUD!)

The following three speeches are from a dramatization of fairy tales by Hans Christian Andersen. The first is from the Tinder Box story and the second and third from the Emperor's New Clothes. The first is essentially for female actors; the third for males; and the second is designed to be played by an actor of either sex. However, it is in the spirit of the exercise that all three speeches could be approached by both male and female actors, and this will be fun to try.

First read the speeches through along with the brief (and obvious) descriptions of the characters. Then perform them using as much exaggeration and imagination as you want. Really have fun with them and imagine that if you were painting rather than acting you would be using a big brush, lots of very bright colours and splashing the paint onto the canvas with enormous brush strokes. Make sure that your instruments of voice and body are fully engaged to their full potential. Inhabit the characters physically, using lots of movement, and vary the volume and tone in your voice as much as possible. However, in doing so, don't forget the previous exercises – make sure that everything you do is instigated and supported by thought and in this way you will remain truthful, albeit in the context of a very exaggerated and expansive style.

Witch (wizened, old, frightening, cackling, loud and stooped)

Good evening my fine, sturdy soldier. How handsome you look in your smart uniform and your sword shining so brightly at your side. I am a kind lady – kind enough to make sure that you are rewarded for the brave deeds that you have done. You shall have as much money as ever you can spend! Would you like that? Well then, listen carefully to me.

Can you see that big tree some way further up the road? Climb to the very top – a simple matter for such a strong, young boy – and then lower yourself down into the trunk … down and down … until you are deep under the tree. There you will find a large underground chamber, which contains all of your future wealth and happiness. Just listen, boy! Once inside you will see three doors. Open the first and you will reveal a large box, full to the brim with copper coins. You may take them all – but beware – the box is guarded by a dog with eyes as big as saucers. He is a fine and noble beast, as fierce as a dog can be. But be not afraid, for he is no match for a brave and pretty soldier. Just look straight into those big eyes of his and command him to stand aside. He will not dare to do else when confronted by such a man as you. But perhaps you would prefer silver? Through the second door lies a box bursting with silver coins. It is guarded by a dog with eyes as big as millstones. He too is as fierce as a dog can be, but fiercer – yet he too will bow to your command. Unless you prefer gold? Through the third door is a box overflowing with gold coins and guarded by a dog who is as fierce as a dog can be, but fiercer. But he will bow to your command if your gaze is firm and your courage holds true. His eyes are as big as the round tower! Go along then, my lovely one. Be brave, true and rich.

Oh, and one more thing. Just a little something that I ask for myself. Not a share of all the riches – what would an old lady want with money? No, my dear – all I ask is this – inside the cavern you will also find a tinderbox: a pathetic, battered object, but it contains an old piece of candle and will suffice to light the way to my poor pauper's bed each lonely night. Bring it to me, boy!

Villain (slimy, toadying, 'very humble', evil and sly)

(To king)

Oh, your majesty – it is known throughout the land that you are a man of taste and great discernment in your choice of wardrobe. The magnificent clothes you wear reflect the wonderful spirit of generosity and flair with which you rule your kingdom. We – humble servant tailors – prostrate ourselves before your colourful and, may I say, divinely attired persona. There can be no doubt that your majesty is the very best dressed king ever. For you, only the very best, sire. We will weave the finest cloth that you could possibly imagine. It will be of a colour and texture that you can only dream of. And from it, we will cut a suit of such heavenly quality that you will swoon to wear it.

But more than all of this – the suit that we will make for you, will be so fine and so delicate, that it will be invisible to all those who are not fit to gaze upon it. Any who are not worthy to hold office in your court, will simply not be able to see it.

Good children's theatre is often large and colourful but still truthful and real.

King (pompous, loud, enthusiastic, corpulent and somewhat effete)

Well, thank you boys! You obviously know a thing or two about fashion. I must admit, I do cut a bit of a dash. Did you say tailors? This is something of a piece of luck. I was thinking of splashing out on something new – something special. I've got a big procession coming up – a right royal do and no mistake – and I haven't got a thing that's suitable. Do you think you could run me something up? I'll pay you well of course. I'm not short of a few bob. How does 10,000 up front sound? So – what can you do for me? I like colour and I like plush. Do you know, I've gone quite flushed with excitement. I'll get my cheque book!

SUBTLE CHARACTERIZATION

Having played with a vivid and extensive 'palette of colours', it is now time to distil this into a more usable characterization technique for our audition purposes. Therefore, to conclude these basic exercises in acting techniques, we will now look at a more subtle form of characterization. However, we must remember that subtlety has many degrees and that some of our monologues will require size, stature and substance; others will require thoughtfulness, feeling and complexity; many will require both; what they will all require is truth!

EXERCISE 4: CHARACTERIZATION B (THOUGHT AND FEELING)

1. Read and digest the following speech. At the moment it is only words, to which you will be required to add character and meaning. Therefore, at the outset, this one speech is suitable for both female and male actors.

Looking back I can see everything so clearly now. In those days I was too full of my own thoughts, my own preoccupations to see the truth. I wasn't aware of what I was doing really … of what I was doing to you. When I finally realized … it was too late! I will never cease to be amazed at my ability for self-deception back then. Well, I certainly paid for it. After you left I just didn't know how to cope. I stopped living and only existed. To be honest, I don't remember too much detail about those days … just the loneliness and the pain … the dreadful ache of missing you. Still, time healed to a certain extent. I moved on – I had to, I suppose. But I never forgot you, and I never stopped loving you. And, if I'm truthful, I never gave up hoping that we would be together again. Now we are … and you're like this … and I realize I've just been fooling myself. We can never go back … life won't let us. Do you remember that day in the park when we first talked about our dreams? Whatever became of them? I squandered mine … and yours too … I'm so sorry.

2. Decide what you think the overall feeling and emotion of the speech should be and, most importantly, invent for yourself a back scenario that would support this. In other words, use your imagination to construct a possible play that this speech might be a part of – what has happened and what has caused the emotion here.

3. Now mark in the places where you believe the feeling may change, develop or intensify. You can use any helpful notation for this – perhaps underlinings with notes at the side, or arrows signifying increases and decreases of feeling. You should also note the changes of energy and new thoughts as you did before.

4. Mark also the part of the speech in which

you are talking directly to another character, and those parts where you are internalizing the feeling more and, as it were, talking to yourself. Stanislavski referred to this as using 'second' and 'first circles of concentration' respectively.

5. Decide how you will stage the piece and where and how you will move if appropriate (you may wish to be still but one move, at least, would add some extra depth to the exercise).

6. Start to rehearse the speech incorporating your notes and decisions. Build up the layers of feeling but do so carefully, so that you

remain truthful and real at all times. Learn it as you go along, so that you can find a final performance that brings it, and the emotions, to natural life.

THE AUDITION SPEECH ITSELF

Let us now look at how you should approach, develop and perfect an audition speech. Remember, by 'perfect', we mean perfect for the purpose – to display a broad and talented 'menu' of skills, not polished perfection. As a broad guide you should tackle each new piece in your repertoire in the following way:

Working on Shakespeare pieces

There is one intrinsic aspect that is fundamental when working upon a Shakespearean speech (and many other 'classical' speeches). This is verse speaking. It is not possible to deal with this in detail here but it is important to set you on a path to some detailed work upon it.

While you should certainly do some additional study in this area, using specialist books upon the subject (there is a volume about performing Shakespeare by this author and publisher), it will be useful to note some basic guidelines here and at this stage.

1. Shakespeare wrote predominantly in verse but not exclusively – prose is used too.
2. The usual and basic form of verse he uses is iambic pentameter: that is, lines of five metrical feet, with each foot consisting of two beats – unstressed/stressed.
3. In addition he makes much use of rhyming couplets and the sonnet form.
4. His use of form is often coupled to character or situation – in very basic terms, verse being used for the more flowery, exalted moments and characters, and prose for the more down-to-earth and pedestrian.
5. The speaking of the verse is fundamentally linked to the meaning – most certainly the two cannot (or at least, should not) be separated. Therefore, you will find the rhythm and flow of the verse a natural aid in your punctuation and shaping of the content.
6. Breathing is all-important to verse speaking. You need plenty of breath and you must be in control of it! Very often the sense of what you are saying will flow through between lines and this requires you to have complete mastery of when and how you breathe.
7. Good diction to shape the lines and meaning is of particular significance too.

1. Read the play thoroughly. You cannot even begin to make decisions about character and situation until you have the required background to the scene and role in question.

2. Do some research on the playwright, including becoming familiar with some of their other works.

3. Start making some observations and decisions about character. Begin by making a list of some general thoughts about them and then progress into thinking about their motivations, objectives and intentions within the scene. Work out their thought processes, the background reasons for them, and the way the scene leads and defines them as it unfolds.

4. Experiment with their physicality, movement and voice (concentrating particularly, for the moment, on movement). It might help you to think about what they might be wearing if the scene were real. You can use the text for this process if it helps but do not be concerned with how you act the piece as yet. Just use some of their words and movements to allow you to begin to get a feel for them as a person, and do not feel pressured to find any kind of an actual performance at this stage. Just relax and see what you can find out about them physically.

5. Repeat this process for their voice particularly. Again, remain relaxed and do not try to perform at this stage – just experiment to find the required tone and modulation. Think obviously about accent but also pay attention to the way they express themselves through the words: concentrate upon their use of vowel sounds and diction and the emphasis they use.

6. Now examine the particular speech and make some decisions as to what you think its importance is: what are the intentions of the author and what particular 'angle' and/or meaning will you be required to emphasize? Think about what you will be trying to do to your audience when you perform it, especially in terms of what you will wish them to think and feel. Try to forget that this is an audition speech at this stage and imagine that it is to be played to an ordinary, paying audience – work out the dynamics of the scene and consider how best to communicate them to your imaginary public.

7. You should now, and only now, begin to rehearse the speech properly, combining the discoveries and decisions you have made. Develop a simple but meaningfully effective 'blocking' for the scene (where you move and at what part of the text), and construct a basic set and setting using chairs (for all necessary furniture) which will, of course, be available at an audition too. Once you have the basic foundations, begin to build and layer your performance. You must remember all of the main concepts involved in what you are trying to do: get the energy of the character and scene just right; make the particular character traits discernible and real; find the period style of the piece (more of this in the next section); establish and develop the meaning and significance of the scene; do justice to the emotions in a truthful and believable manner; and, most importantly of all, tell the 'story' of the piece in as dynamic and engaging a way as possible.

8. As a final check before using the speech at an audition, ensure that you are doing two fundamental things with it. Firstly, are you doing the text and the author's intentions justice? Secondly, are you doing yourself and the talents you possess justice? Make certain that you can say 'yes' to both of these very important questions.

Work hard so that you always do yourself justice.

STYLE AND PERIOD

This is such an important aspect of your audition speech preparation that it needs to be looked at a little in isolation. Many actors, both during auditions and when performing, fail because they ignore, or do not focus enough upon, this vital element of the material they are using.

In terms of modern pieces you will be primarily concerned with the physical and vocal attributes associated with the character's environment and class. However, in period pieces, you will need to think about not only these aspects but also the particular style attributed to the time. Very often, a play will fundamentally embrace a very specific style and the whole playing of it will be firmly rooted in its adroit execution. One thinks especially of playwrights like Coward, Wilde and all of the Restoration writers, but every worthy and important playwright will require a certain style founded in content, period, class, or 'manners' of some kind.

Therefore, when working on an audition speech always subject it, and the play it comes from, to scrutiny in terms of style. Think about the period in which it is set, the environment in which it takes place, the class of society in which it is rooted, and any particular physical and vocal manners that are required as a result of all of these. Then ask yourself questions about movement and voice appropriately: what is your posture, how should you move, how should you speak, what affectations do you need and why? Practise these and let them become fully incorporated into your performance.

In order to be a little more specific about this process, try the following exercise:

EXERCISE 5: VOCAL AND PHYSICAL STYLE

1. Select any audition speech, but preferably one set in a specific period, and one that you are likely to incorporate into your repertoire.
2. Investigate and decide about the costume that the character would be wearing during this speech. Be specific here and think in detail. For women include the undergarments as these are often of significance in terms of movement. Don't forget the footwear, as this is of vital importance too.
3. Assemble this costume as much as you possibly can – either from similar garments that you may own or from second-hand and charity shops. You may be able to be accurate if dealing with a recent period, but if not, use the best possible equivalents that you can find. Essentially you should be looking to recreate the feel and essence of the costume.
4. Wearing the costume, experiment with the way it makes you feel. Think about how it is

Thinking about period and style is vital.

leading you to stand and move. Focus particu-larly upon the restrictions it may place upon you physically – particularly that underwear!

5. Incorporate into this your knowledge of the class and period and think about what is important to the character in terms of the society in which they exist.

6. Now play the speech in costume, and after you have learned it (it is difficult to explore physical style with a book in your hand), let your body and voice naturally and intuitively find the style. Having found it, embrace and enjoy it; let it develop and have life. Remem-ber all the time about the image and impres-sion that the character would be creating for themselves, and to what degree they would wish to conform to the rules of their society and environment.

7. Finish by performing the speech out of costume (as you will at an audition – albeit dressed somewhat appropriately), but try to continue the feel of it, and the effect it has upon you, through your imagination.

8 The audition itself

PERSONAL APPEAL

It may sound obvious, but do make sure that you are friendly and polite to the people who are auditioning you. One of these people will (in most cases) be the director and it is a much overlooked fact that, as well as wanting to cast somebody who is right for the part both in terms of talent and suitability for the role, they will also be concerned to employ someone who they feel will be easy and rewarding to work with. Try to put yourself in their shoes for a moment: all the talent in the world will not seem that appealing to you if you are afraid that the rehearsal period will be a nightmare of personal conflict and lack of unity.

You may well be thinking that this is a given: why on earth would you not be friendly and polite? You would have a good point but, amazingly, it can happen, and there are reasons for this. It may simply be that the performer is in an inescapably bad mood, due to a row with their partner that morning, perhaps, or a difficult journey to the audition. However, the main two reasons why you might not appear as personable and warm as you should are, firstly, a lack of confidence and, secondly, nerves – which can give the false impression of your being distant and aloof, and having too much confidence – this can frighten the director into thinking that you will be arrogant and all too ready to undermine them in the rehearsal room. Therefore, try to avoid these two contrasting but equally unhelpful states of mind and be your usual cheerful, positive, yet respectful self, even though nervousness may try to impede you in this.

DIRECTORS AND PRODUCERS ARE HUMAN TOO

When performers think about the process of auditioning, they usually conjure up a certain picture in their mind concerning the power balance between themselves and the directors and producers who might be auditioning them. They see themselves as the vulnerable and pathetically hopeful underdog, at the mercy of those mighty ogres who might wish to employ them. They view these potential employers as the ones who have all the power and none of the problems of the casting process. However, in reality, this is simply not the case: the director may feel just as nervous as you and will almost certainly feel as vulnerable. Remember that they are human: they will be concerned about things such as what you think of them, how worthy you consider the project or the company, and what they say and how they present themselves.

OPPOSITE: **Try to build a strong repertoire of audition pieces.**

When auditioning you must appear easy to work with, as this can be as important as your talent.

A MATTER OF OPINION

During the course of most auditions there will be an opportunity for you to interact with the director in some way. There may well be an interview element to the audition when they try to find out a little more about you and the kind of work you have done in the past, and tell you about the production and something of what to expect if you are chosen for the job. It may also come in the form of actual direction –they may brief you about the scene you are to read or, when applicable, ask you to perform your audition pieces in a particular way. Whatever form the interaction may take, it is important that you make some contribution to the process that is not just compliance. Try to reveal the

way you think, give your opinion on what is being talked about, and make sure that they see that you are interested and engaged with the project. On the other hand, keep your contribution constructive and modest, and guard against being over-opinionated or confrontational. Certainly you do not what to appear a 'yes' person – totally passive, compliant and vacuous; neither do you want to appear challenging or difficult, so keep your opinions constructive, respectful and moderate.

An example of poor personal interaction with a director at an audition might be as follows: a director is casting a Shakespeare play and asks an actor to sightread a speech from the text or perform a prepared one. This particular director is keen that their production should be modern, accessible and relevant, and (rightly or wrongly) they want to achieve this by focusing more upon the meaning of the text and less upon the poetry and verse rhythms in particular. Therefore they ask the actor to do the speech again but, this time, to disregard the rhythm, metre and verse structure as entirely as possible and speak it as if it were actually written in prose. The actor thinks that this is a totally misguided approach and in response to this requested 'prosification' says baldly something to the effect of, 'But it's not written like that!'

This has achieved nothing, except almost certainly losing the actor the job. While a director should, in theory, be able to accept a challenge such as this and respond to it positively, in practice they are, as we have already noted, only human

and this direct challenge to their opinion and authority will almost certainly prompt them to feel undermined and not disposed to working with an actor who might be equally confrontational and opinionated in rehearsal.

From the actor's point of view the encounter will be just as negative. It may well be that they value their own opinions, that they are passionate about Shakespearean verse speaking and felt they needed to make their point. Indeed, they have a perfect right to make their feelings known but, if they are going to do so in such a way at an audition, when they have not yet been offered the job, then what was the point of coming in the first place?

Of course much of the problem here is in the way the opinion has been stated. Had the actor engaged the director in a more positive conversa-

Do not be confrontational when discussing the role.

tion, exploring the point rather than rejecting it, then this might have been better, even helpful. However, to show disagreement with a negative attitude towards any aspect of the audition is to waste your time – directors will not want to work with you, however talented you may be. Engage with the director's ideas certainly, but do not show contempt for them – even mildly. If you really don't like the director or the way in which they are planning to direct the play, then you can simply decline the job when offered, but there is no point in 'closing the door' for the future – always leave an audition having given a good impression of all aspects of your work and personality.

ENTERING THE AUDITION ROOM

Just before you are about to enter the audition room and meet the director, producers or whoever may be auditioning you, remember to summon up a positive attitude. First impressions are vitally important in all walks of life and never more so than in a casting situation. Therefore, you will want to be at your best – not artificially exuberant and effusive – but just simply yourself, displaying your personality in an open and generous way. The best way to achieve this is to banish all the negative thoughts that surround an audition – thoughts which might otherwise inhibit and distort your natural ability to present yourself in a flattering and engaging way. Positive thinking ultimately leads to relaxation: not a passive, lacklustre and insipid relaxation, but proper relaxation, which allows the body and mind to operate without unnecessary tensions and so fulfil the potential of personality.

As far as auditions are concerned this is, unfortunately, easier said than done! Their competitive nature, the likelihood of failure and the very process of being critically examined both professionally and personally all have a propensity for leading you towards a negative attitude. For this reason you must view positive thinking as not just a preferable state of mind which, with fingers crossed might just possibly be achieved when 'the wind is in the right direction', but as part of your professional remit when you audition. It should be an essential, the attainment of which must be analysed and practised as part of your overall technique.

There are two factors that must underline this 'Positive Thinking Technique' for you. The first is to remember that auditioning is a 'numbers game'. As we have already examined in this book, the odds of being successful in one audition are considerably less favourable than those of several and, thus, any one audition must be seen as part of your development towards success – not necessarily yielding fruits on its own. This will help take the pressure off the particular occasion and allow you to think of it as just another part of your job.

The second, and most important, factor is the fundamental necessity for you to believe in yourself. However hard and daunting the task may be you must be determined in your belief that you have the necessary weapons to succeed, albeit in the end! You must focus upon your strengths and, while not ignoring your weaknesses (for to discount them would be never to eradicate them), allow all of the talent within you (and the craft that you have practised so hard in order to release that talent) to have prime importance in your truthful opinion of yourself. Of course, this must be a deep-seated confidence and not just rhetoric: you must truly believe in your ability and not just be self-deceiving in the hope of convincing yourself sufficiently to banish doubt for a few moments of time. This comes down, once again, to the inescapable necessity of testing your vocation. If you have not done (or are not doing) this sufficiently then you will have no real basis for genuine confidence in yourself as a professional performer, however much you may pretend such

Auditioning is a two-way process

Applying for a job as a performer in professional theatre is often regarded in the following, rather erroneous, way: the performer, working within a profession where unemployment is rife, is desperate for the job and wants it at any price, quite regardless of what it may be, who it is working for, where it is, the amount of remuneration being offered and how it is to be staged. The director or producer, on the other hand, is the party with all the choice – they will offer the job if the performer is talented enough, fits the casting brief, has an appealing personality, seems as if they will work hard and various other criteria both real or imagined by the anxious and 'humble' performer.

This really should not be, and in fact is not, the case. We have already explored how you should be careful to give the right impression at an audition and to ensure that you do not unnecessarily limit your chances by poor communication skills, but this does not mean to say that you should see yourself as an 'Oliver Twist' type of character – begging for 'scraps' from the director's table. Far from it – auditioning should be viewed as a two-way process, equal in its decision-making process between both parties. That is to say, while those who are auditioning you are deciding whether you are right for the job, so you are deciding whether or not the job is right for you.

Although your attitude should be to find and keep work in general, this does not mean to say that every job will be automatically appealing and has to be taken at all costs. It may be, on some occasions, that an aspect of the potential employment will not be to your liking and, although your work ethic should dictate that turning down work should happen rarely and only when strictly necessary, it is worth remembering that you have a decision-making role here too, as well as the director and producers.

The biggest culprits in terms of seeing auditioning as a one-way street are the employers themselves within the industry. They either forget that the performer has a choice or, even worse, they ignore or do not recognize the fact and assume that everyone whom they audition will be desperate to work for them at any 'price'. Although this may often be the case, to assume it and deny the performer respect in this way is arrogance, albeit often unintentionally so. In the same way, for a performer to adopt such a view of what they are doing is to be unnecessarily complicit in an unbalanced power struggle.

A far more balanced and healthy attitude and approach to the casting process, for both parties, is to consider it a meeting of potential partners in the enterprise: the producer has a job to offer that might be suitable for the performer and, in return, the performer brings their talents, abilities, experience and personalities 'to the table' to see if they are suitable for the producer. This really is the case, no matter how much the ego on the one hand and the need for work on the other may seem to deny it and, even if you are in truth yearning to get the part, it is an attitude and approach that will allow you to be less anxious and give you a sense of greater control over your destiny.

confidence to others and yourself. If you have done this sufficiently then you will have earned the right to assume your worthiness to look for work generally and any individual audition specifically, and you will find this very deep-seated and fundamental belief in yourself, however bad, difficult and discouraging your life as a theatrical jobseeker may become.

So as you walk into an audition room to meet 'the panel', and if you have earned the right to do so (and only if), and if you have guarded against arrogance, then walk tall and think of yourself as a huge potential asset to their production which they would be foolish to reject but, if they do, will simply allow another manage-

ment to benefit from their mistake. This is not only the key to much more successful auditioning but to a less stressful and overwhelming experience too.

SIGHTREADING FROM THE SCRIPT

We have already established elsewhere that the most common form of auditioning in modern times is the reading of an extract from the play that is to be produced. Therefore, one of your main tasks as a professional performer is to make sure that you are as skilled and adept at this as possible. Obviously, this method of casting does not afford you as much opportunity for preparation and readiness

It is important to believe in yourself and be confident in your abilities.

as when audition speeches were usually at least part of the experience. However, there is still much that you can do to develop your skills in this area.

Your first consideration should be to read the play prior to the audition. Of course, this may simply be impossible, for a number of possible reasons: you may not have time (sometimes notice to attend auditions is very short and, even with today's quick online delivery services, you might not be able to obtain a copy fast enough); the play might not be in print; it might be a new work (still only in the possession of the writer, director and producer); you may not have been able to find out what the play is at all (a likely and often repeated event in the 'hurly burly' of casting). On the other hand, if you are able to get hold of it in sufficient time, then a good, long study of it will reap huge rewards – not only to prepare you for reading any one part of it, but in order to allow you to make positive and insightful contributions to any discussion that may ensue.

If possible, try to rehearse some of it too. It may be impractical for you to do this with the whole role if it is a large one, but reading just some of it aloud and 'playing' with various different ways of expressing the text will help enormously when it comes to the audition itself. It does not matter if you focus upon a scene that is not chosen at the audition – any specific work will have a general effect to the good. Try not to be too determined in the way you practise the part though, so that you are ready to accept any direction before or during the actual reading process.

You may feel, in light of the fact that statistically you are more likely to fail at the audition than to succeed (although of course every audition is a learning process and a chance to meet new contacts), that this type of preparation is a potential waste of time. If this is your attitude then it could not be further from the truth: reading and exploring a play that is new to you (or even revisiting one that was previously familiar) is always a worthwhile endeavour. It will not only increase your depth of knowledge in terms of dramatic literature generally, but add another possibility for audition material for the future.

Having done as much preparation as possible you will now want to give as good a reading as possible at the audition itself. A good director will talk you through the extract that you are going to be asked to read, for it is in their interest to ensure that you understand what the scene is about and what is required of you. However, as they may have repeated this process of instruction many times during the day they may not always be as detailed or as clear as they might wish to be. Therefore, do not be afraid to ask questions. This not only helps to show that you care and are interested, but the more informed you are about a scene the better. Don't overdo this – you will not be thanked for unduly elongating an already time-consuming process for them – but, on the other hand, make sure that you gather sufficient insight to achieve a credible and intelligent reading.

When it comes to the reading itself, a word of warning: although you may be asked to read a monologue from the play, it is more likely that it will be a duologue at least. If this is the case someone else at the audition will 'read in' the other part(s). There may be another actor appointed to do this – perhaps someone who, for whatever reason, has already been cast in the production – but, more often or not, the task will be performed by one of the audition panel: perhaps even the director. Of, course, whoever does read with you may also be an actor and, in this case, you will be able to interact with them and 'bounce off' their energy and expression. However, if they are not, then there is likely to be little chance of meaningful interplay of any sort. This will leave you with the tricky job of giving an intelligent, thoughtful and emotional interpretation, while talking to

Be brave when sight reading and really 'go for it'!

another character whose dialogue may be without shape, appropriate intonation, colour, timing and, at worst, may be delivered in a monotone. To make this worse, the person will probably be distracted, either by analysing your performance or the practical considerations of the occasion (timekeeping and who is next on the list, for instance), so you will need to be prepared for lack of fluency, inappropriate pauses and inaccuracy of text. They may not only be poor actors but poor readers as well and this will exacerbate the problem still further.

It is extraordinary that producers, who are taking time and spending money in trying to cast the best and most appropriate performers for the job, should seriously hamper the process by expecting them to give their best in a situation akin to reading plays in class when at school – completely deprived of the usual, and essential, interplay and reaction that is fundamental to creating a believable, truthful and expressive performance. However, you will come up against this situation more often than you might think. There is little that you can actually do to remedy the situation other than be

Move

Always get up and move around when reading from a script at an audition. If the director is at all competent she or he will want you to do this anyway and make facility for it. However, if not, ask if you can 'move' the piece rather than just read it. Even if it is a static scene from a sitting position, move your chair out into the room and create 'space' for the scene.

In the same way, remember to create the character physically as well as vocally. When reading a script it is very easy to see it as something of an intellectual exercise that is just about words and how they are said. However, you must take these words and begin to give an indication of character and reaction to situation from them – this must be done with the whole of you and not just the voice.

prepared for it and to rely on your own inner impetus and inspiration. Try to listen to just the words, rather than the actor as you would normally do, and create a reaction in yourself directly from the page and the playwright, rather than from the other performance.

The most important consideration when sightreading at auditions is the fact that you will not usually get a second go at it, so you have to produce something worthwhile at the first attempt. You need not worry about polish or perfection here, but you must make sure that you provide plenty of indication of the way you would play the part were you to be cast, and the skills and talents that you would bring to it. The key to doing this is not to be in any way hesitant or restrained. You will have had at least some chance to make decisions about how the extract should be performed (even if it has only been a quick glance and fleeting explanation as they hand you the script), so you must take your courage in your hands and really 'go for it'! Remember, there are no second prizes in this game and caution will not serve you well here. It is far better to be bold and get it wrong than to fail to demonstrate what is actually there. Auditioning is a risky business but it will

not surrender its rewards if you shy away from the danger. It will be easy for you to make the excuse that you do not really know the play and therefore you can only be expected to do your best and explore around the edges of the part. This attitude will not be shared by the audition panel and, however unreasonably, they will expect you to produce some high-quality and enthralling 'goods'.

EXERCISES IN SIGHTREADING FOR AUDITIONS

The following exercises will help to prepare you for the process of auditioning and 'cold' readings. Use them in the comfort and security of your own home, to prepare yourself as much as possible for being bold and imaginative with material in auditions.

EXERCISE 1: UNKNOWN SCRIPT WITH NOTICE

1.   Imagine that you have been sent or emailed the segment of script following these instructions. It is from a new play by a little-known

playwright called Bill Shakespeare and you have not been given any information about it. Therefore, you only have the scene itself in order to make performance decisions. As you will see, there is a male and female character in this scene and the one appropriate to your sex will be the one you must imagine you are auditioning for.

2. Work on the scene as much as possible but within a three-hour time constraint. This will vaguely replicate the situation, were you to have been sent it a day or two in advance and remembering that you will have other things to do in your life as well as prepare for an audition. You may use the time in one session or break it up. If you can find a friend or colleague to work on the other part with you then so much the better.

3. You may work on the script in any way you wish – but it might help you to apply the methods used for audition pieces in Chapter 7 as a general guide.

4. Think about the following basic points as you work – the second will be particularly relevant for this 'new' writer:

- character – vocal and physical;
- thought process and understanding;
- situation;
- emotion;
- interaction with the other character;
- the shape of the scene;
- the pace of the scene and how it changes; and
- the energy and power of the scene.

Exeunt all but BENEDICK and BEATRICE

BENEDICK
Lady Beatrice, have you wept all this while?

BEATRICE
Yea, and I will weep a while longer.

BENEDICK
I will not desire that.

BEATRICE
You have no reason; I do it freely.

BENEDICK
Surely I do believe your fair cousin is wronged.

BEATRICE
Ah, how much might the man deserve of me that would right her!

BENEDICK
Is there any way to show such friendship?

BEATRICE
A very even way, but no such friend.

BENEDICK
May a man do it?

BEATRICE
It is a man's office, but not yours.

BENEDICK
I do love nothing in the world so well as you: is not that strange?

BEATRICE
As strange as the thing I know not. It were as possible for me to say I loved nothing so well as you: but believe me not; and yet I lie not; I confess nothing, no I deny nothing. I am sorry for my cousin.

BENEDICK
By my sword, Beatrice, thou lovest me.

BEATRICE
Do not swear by it, and eat it.

BENEDICK
I will swear by it that you love me; and I will make him eat it that says I love not you.

BEATRICE
Will you not eat your word?

BENEDICK
With no sauce that can be devised to it. I protest I love thee.

BEATRICE
Why, then, God forgive me!

BENEDICK
What offence, sweet Beatrice?

BEATRICE

You have stayed me in a happy hour: I was about to protest I loved you.

BENEDICK

And do it with all thy heart.

BEATRICE

I love you with so much of my heart that none is left to protest.

BENEDICK

Come, bid me do any thing for thee.

BEATRICE

Kill Claudio.

BENEDICK

Ha! Not for the wide world.

BEATRICE

You kill me to deny it. Farewell.

BENEDICK

Tarry, sweet Beatrice.

BEATRICE

I am gone, though I am here: there is no love in you: nay, I pray you, let me go.

BENEDICK

Beatrice, —

BEATRICE

In faith, I will go.

BENEDICK

We'll be friends first.

BEATRICE

You dare easier be friends with me than fight with mine enemy.

BENEDICK

Is Claudio thine enemy?

BEATRICE

Is he not approved in the height a villain, that hath slandered, scorned, dishonoured my kinswoman? O that I were a man! What, bear her in hand until they come to take hands; and then, with public accusation, uncovered slander, unmitigated rancour, — O God, that I were a man! I would eat his heart in the market-place.

BENEDICK

Hear me, Beatrice, —

BEATRICE

Talk with a man out at a window? A proper saying!

BENEDICK

Nay, but, Beatrice, —

BEATRICE

Sweet Hero! She is wronged, she is slandered, she is undone.

BENEDICK

Beat—

BEATRICE

Princes and counties! Surely, a princely testimony, a goodly count, Count Comfect; a sweet gallant, surely! O that I were a man for his sake! or that I had any friend would be a man for my sake! But manhood is melted into courtesies, valour into compliment, and men are only turned into tongue, and trim ones too: he is now as valiant as Hercules that only tells a lie and swears it. I cannot be a man with wishing, therefore I will die a woman with grieving.

BENEDICK

Tarry, good Beatrice. By this hand, I love thee.

BEATRICE

Use it for my love some other way than swearing by it.

BENEDICK

Think you in your soul the Count Claudio hath wronged Hero?

BEATRICE

Yea, as sure as I have a thought or a soul.

BENEDICK

Enough, I am engaged; I will challenge him. I will kiss your hand, and so I leave you. By this hand, Claudio shall render me a dear account. As you hear of me, so think of me. Go, comfort your cousin: I must say she is dead: and so, farewell.

Bedroom Farce is an excellent comedy for studying technique.

EXERCISE 2: KNOWN SCRIPT WITH NOTICE

1. Imagine that you know that you will be auditioning for the comedy play Bedroom Farce by Alan Ayckbourn.
2. Obtain a copy of the play from a shop or library and read it thoroughly.
3. This play contains a lot of duologue scenes between male and female characters. There is an older couple (Delia and Ernest), as well as younger characters. Pick an appropriate scene and focus upon the character of your sex as one that you have been told you will be auditioning for.
4. Work on the scene as much as possible but within a three-hour time constraint. This will vaguely replicate the situation, were you to have been informed about it a day or two in advance and remembering that you will have other things to do in your life as well as prepare for an audition. You may use the time in one session or break it up. If you can find a friend or colleague to work on the other part with you then so much the better.
5. You may work on the script in any way you wish – but it might help you to apply the methods used for audition pieces in Chapter 7 as a general guide.
6. Think about the following basic points as you work:

OPPOSITE: You will often audition for children's theatre, which will be fun and exciting.

- character – vocal and physical;
- thought process;
- situation;
- emotion;
- interaction with the other character;
- the shape of the scene and its comedy;
- the pace of the scene and how it changes; and
- the energy and power of the scene.

EXERCISE 3: UNKNOWN SCRIPT WITH (ALMOST) NO NOTICE

1. Imagine that you have arrived at an audition and are presented with the script (this follows the instructions for this exercise) for the first time and without any prior knowledge of it. In order to mirror a specific type of audition that you may often attend, it is an extract from a Christmas play for young children and their families. It also includes a lot of movement and 'business', especially at the beginning. Both men and women can audition for the part of the Elf, but older actors might like to be Father Christmas.

2. The imaginary audition is running late and the director has no time to tell you anything about it at all (this is unlikely, but let us work to the 'worst case scenario'). However, you are given it in the waiting room fifteen minutes before you are called in to the auditioning room. You have only the dialogue and the stage directions to help you.

3. Work on the scene but strictly limit yourself to fifteen minutes from first starting to read it. Do as much as you can in this very short time. If you can, work with a friend or colleague so that you can perform/read the scene after the time limit and see how you get on. You must stick to the rules if this is to be a useful exercise though.

4. You may work on the script in any way you wish – but it might help you to apply the methods used for audition pieces in Chapter 7 as a general guide.

5. Think about the following basic points as you work – the last point is very important in this situation:

- character – vocal and physical;
- thought process;
- situation;
- emotion;
- interaction with the other character;
- the shape of the scene;
- the pace of the scene and how it changes;
- the energy and power of the scene; and
- the mime, physicality and 'business' involved in the scene.

6. Now work on the scene again but within the constraints of Exercise 1. This will not only give you a more thorough interaction with the scene but help you to evaluate your performance within very different preparation scenarios.

The Night Before Christmas

As the Curtain rises we find ourselves in the Basement Factory at Father Christmas HQ.

FC's Chief Elf is sprawled in FC's special chair listening (with his eyes closed) to an ipod and singing along loudly and tunelessly. At the same time, toys are spewing out of the Toy Making Machine and piling on the floor. The machine is noisy and, as each toy comes out, it makes a burping sound. As the last toy emerges the machine makes an awful sound and stops. There is also the continuing sound of a large clock ticking. The Elf is unaware of the internal telephone which is ringing and flashing incessantly. He opens his eyes lazily and, seeing the flashing light for the first time, rushes in panic to the phone.

ELF (*very nervous*)

Hello! Yes, Father Christmas! No, Father Christmas! I really am working very hard, Father Christmas. Pardon, Father Christmas? … Yes, I do know that it's Christmas Eve … Yes, I do know you want to load up your sleigh … the toy-making machine has just got a bit stuck, that's all … I'll soon have it working again … Yes, Father Christmas, I'll start sending the toys up again right away.

He puts down the phone and dashes to the pile of toys. He bundles half of the toys into the dumb-waiter-like lift. The others he quickly hides in a secret compartment inside FC's chair. He looks very guilty as he does this. He shuts the lift and presses a button. We hear the sound of the lift ascending. He then turns to the outlet of the machine and looks deep inside to see why no more toys are coming out.

ELF

Oh bother! What can be wrong with this stupid machine?

ELF (*shouts up the outlet*)

You must make more toys!

ELF (*looks round at the audience*)

Oh, no wonder! Why are you all just sitting there? You silly little Elves … you are supposed to be working the machine. I can't run the whole factory by myself, you know! How many times do I have to tell you? … Right, for the last time … and listen carefully – all you elves here pull the levers, like this.

He shows one third of the audience. (The following audience participation can be changed and embellished as required).

ELF

And you elves must turn the wheels.

He shows another third.

ELF

And you elves over here must pull the ropes.

He shows the final third.

ELF

So are you all ready?

AUDIENCE (*Hesitantly*)

Yes!

ELF

I didn't hear that. You must say 'Yes, Chief Elf' and salute. So … are you ready?

AUDIENCE (*they salute*)

Yes, Chief Elf!

ELF

That's better. Now remember this – whenever I ask you a question you always say, 'Yes, Chief Elf!' or 'No, Chief Elf!' and salute at the same time. Will you remember that?

AUDIENCE

Yes, Chief Elf! (They salute, encouraged by Elf)

ELF

Good! Is it Christmas?

AUDIENCE

Yes, Chief Elf!

ELF

Are you excited?

AUDIENCE

Yes, Chief Elf!

ELF

Would you rather be at school?

AUDIENCE

No, Chief Elf!

ELF

Have no fun and games at all?

AUDIENCE

No, Chief Elf!

ELF

Is Christmas morning getting near?

AUDIENCE

Yes, Chief Elf!

ELF

Have you all been good this year?

AUDIENCE

Yes, Chief Elf!

ELF

Do your parents all agree with that?

AUDIENCE

No, Chief Elf!

ELF

Would you like some presents from Father Christmas?

AUDIENCE

Yes, Chief Elf!

ELF

Well, I'm keeping lots of presents just for me. Here we go then … one two three … machine work!

He pushes a button. The machine noise starts again and the elf encourages the audience in their actions. The toys begin to appear again and the elf starts frantically sending some up in the lift but hiding others in the chair as before. After a while the machine noise suddenly stops again and there is a loud siren noise.

ELF (*in a panic again*)

Stop working, everyone. Something is happening.

ELECTRONIC VOICE

Warning, Warning! Toy machine automatic cut-off has been activated. Father Christmas is approaching the factory. Father Christmas is approaching the factory.

ELF

Father Christmas? But he never comes down here.

At this point all noise stops and, with a loud cry, FC enters via the Santa Chute.

FC

Oh deary, deary me! I really must get some stairs put in

ELF

Are you all right, Father Christmas?

FC

Yes, yes, my friend – I'm fine. Help me up, would you!

The Elf does so

FC

Thank you. So, my faithful little Chief Elf, how are you?

ELF

I'm very well thank you, Father Christmas.

FC

Jolly good! (*Turning to the audience*) And hello to you little elves. How lovely to see you all. I hope that you have been working hard.

ELF (*quickly*)

Oh yes they have, Father Christmas. (To the audience) Haven't you?

AUDIENCE

Yes, Chief Elf! (*They salute, encouraged by Elf*)

ELF

You don't ever want to stop working, do you?

AUDIENCE

No, Chief Elf! (*They salute. Some may say yes, which will embarrass the Elf.*)

FC

Well done! But from tomorrow you will all be able to have a rest. It's Christmas Eve – time for me to deliver all the toys to all the girls and boys.

ELF

Why?

FC

Pardon?

ELF

Why do you have to do that every year? Give all the toys we make to all the girls and boys. Why don't we keep them all?

FC
Because it's my job to give presents to people. I love making people happy. It's what I do … and it's your job to help me.

ELF (*sulkily*)
I see!

FC
And that is what I have come down here to talk to you about.
FC goes to his chair and sits on the Elf's iPod which is left there. FC jumps quickly up.

FC
Ahhhh!
The Elf grabs the iPod and hurriedly chucks it into the machine. FC settles himself and continues:

FC
You don't seem to be making enough toys. At least, not enough are coming up in the lift … my sleigh is only half full. I must set off on my rounds soon if I'm to be finished by morning but I can't leave unless I have all toys for all the girls and boys. Is there a problem with the machine?
During the following the Elf (much to his dismay) can't seem to help giving himself away, and FC gradually gets suspicious.

ELF
Don't worry, Father Christmas. I'll soon get to the bottom of it.

FC
Good!

ELF
It won't take me long to get to the seat of the problem.

FC
Good!

ELF
I'm sure you're sitting on the solution.

FC
Am I?
He gets up, examines his seat and finds
the secret store. The Elf turns away in shame.

FC
What are all these toys doing in here.?

ELF
What toys, in where?

FC
These toys in here.

ELF
Oh, those toys in there.

FC
Yes!

ELF
They're mine.

FC
Yours? But these are toys from the machine.

ELF (*suddenly blurting out*)
Well, I don't think it's right to give all the toys away. I don't like giving. Christmas is stupid. Why give someone a present when you can keep it for yourself?

FC
Have you been hiding some of the toys, so that you can keep them?

ELF
Yes! I had to. If I left it to you, you'd give them all away.

FC
Well yes, of course I would. Elf, I think it's about time you and I had a little talk … about Christmas.

ELF
I know all about Christmas … it's a waste of time … it's kids stuff!

FC
Oh, you silly sausage! Come and sit down here by me.
The Elf reluctantly does so.

FC
Now, I want to tell you a little story about Christmas.

Auditioning for film and TV

These days, many of the auditions that you attend as a professional performer will be for television and, to a lesser extent, film. On these occasions you will almost certainly be reading from the script in question. Although your basic approach in terms of your performance should be the same, you should consider in particular the following points:

1. The most fundamental difference between stage and screen acting is that the former needs to be projected (both in terms of volume and size of performance) and the latter does not – the camera and the microphone come to the performer rather than the reverse. Screen acting is often perceived to be more truthful and more detailed and 'smaller' in its execution. This is not always the case but it is certainly needs to be less projected and artificially expansive.

2. Performing for the camera often requires the practitioner to move, turn and, even, look in very precise and directed ways in order to comply with the shot angles and camera positions needed. This means that, as a performer, you may find yourself needing to couple truthful and natural acting with artificial requirements that may not necessarily spring from the situation (as on stage), and which need to be incorporated into the spontaneity of your work. You will also often need to be in awkward positions, perhaps nearer to someone that you are talking to than would normally be natural, in order to accommodate the all-powerful camera's requirements!

3. Particularly in terms of commercial castings you will often be asked to focus on very specific actions or reactions that can be isolated from the normal acting process and seem extremely inorganic. For example, in a hypothetical audition for a coffee advertisement, say, you might be instructed by the director to sip a cup of an inferior brew and then show by your facial expression (in close-up) that you dislike this intensely but are trying to pretend that it is delicious because it is cheaper than your usual blend.

Exercise

Select one of your audition speeches and ask a friend or colleague to direct you in it and to give you very detailed movements and reactions – even turns of the head and eye focus should be included. Find ways to make these work naturally within your thought processes. For instance, if you are required to turn your head in a certain direction on a particular word, incorporate a reason for this in the thought that triggers the line – not wanting another character to see your face at that moment perhaps.

ELF

I don't like stories anymore – they're for children.

FC

But you like *telling* stories, don't you?

ELF

Oh yes, I like telling stories … and I'm very good at it.

FC

That's right – you are … so you can help me tell the story.

ELF

How can I help you tell the story when I don't know what it is?

FC

Well you can just join in, as we go along.

ELF

But we haven't got time for stories. We're very busy.

FC

Ah well, I can do something about that.

ELF

What?

FC

I can control time.

ELF (*impressed*)

Can you?

FC

Why of course. How do you think I manage to get so much done in just one night …? I can stop time whenever I like. So I will stop time while we tell the story. Like this.

He clicks his fingers and the noise of ticking stops as the lights change.

9 Recalls and workshop auditions

Very often those who are casting are not able to make a decision after just one 'round' of auditions and decide to use an elimination process by 'recalling' those who have interested them. Often this will just be once before the decisions are then made but sometimes (especially for the more important casting assignments) there may well be several recalls – gradually reducing the 'hopefuls' to perhaps just two for the final round. Thus, you may find yourself in the position of attending more than one audition for the same job or role.

Obviously the best result of any audition is to be told that you have secured the part, but the next best thing is to be recalled. It is certainly a very positive step forward in your quest to secure a particular part and it should be embraced positively and with enthusiasm, but be careful that you do not ignore the basic rule of auditioning and start to become too emotionally attached to the idea of success at this stage. Whilst it is extremely good news to secure a recall, the bad news is amplified in equal measure if rejection follows, so do not allow yourself to become too hopeful too early – stay positive but realistic and keep the champagne on ice just for now! If you are lucky enough (or unlucky enough – depending upon the outcome) to be involved in one of the audition processes in which you are 'whittled down' to just a few from a large number of performers, then you should be even more careful to guard against disappointment while embracing the encouragement of your success at the same time.

THE WORKSHOP AUDITION

Recall auditions often take the form of 'workshop' sessions, as explored in this chapter. However, it is not unusual for directors to take an opposite approach and begin with a workshop from which they then select certain performers for individual recalls.

Auditioning itself can be a lonely affair and, considering that performing itself is usually such a team activity, it can seem rather unnatural and remote from the abilities it endeavours to test: you will often find yourself performing a scene in which you pretend other performers and audience are present, or reading from a script you have only just seen and interacting with perhaps a member of the production team or whoever may have been co-opted as reader of the part you are to play opposite.

Conversely, the workshop audition is, by its very nature, a much more fundamental and organic approach to casting and selection. Here you will work with a group of people, all of whom are, like you, hopeful of securing a particular job. In some instances they might be under consideration for the same part as you; in others they might be

OPPOSITE: Auditions should be a meeting of potential partners.

candidates for other parts that may or may not interact with yours in the work. Whatever the situation, this type of audition should be seen by you as an opportunity to display your talents in the way they are meant to function: within a team environment and subject to plenty of interplay and interaction. They can, by their nature, seem quite daunting but are a perfect chance for you to engage all of your abilities and skills in a far more natural and harmonious way.

There are some pitfalls to be avoided here and the most dangerous is the tendency to view the process competitively. One of the fundamentals being tested in this type of audition is your ability to work as an ensemble member of a cast so, even though you will be aware that there are almost certainly more participants than parts on offer, you should view your fellow participants not as competitors but more as comrades.

Therefore, remember to apply all of the normal rules for performance work: listen to and respect the contribution of the others; feed off their input and allow it to inform and enrich your own endeavour; share your energy with them and match their enthusiasm; and make sure that you work with their ideas as well as your own – harmonizing the two if possible.

Another pitfall, connected to the first, is the difficulty of finding the right balance between adequate and productive involvement on the one hand and a dominant and overbearing approach on the other. It may help to realize that, of these

Accept and build when improvising and be inventive.

two opposites, the former is more damaging than the latter: this is an audition and you must make sure that you are noticed and that your skills are given ample chance to shine. Therefore, make sure, above all else, that you do not 'sit on the sidelines' in a workshop audition. Try to be consistently involved and proactive in the work that you are asked to do, and give those who are auditioning the opportunity to see not only your talents and abilities but your readiness to participate fully in the work and endeavours of a team. Remember, auditions are hard to get and each one is a precious opportunity for the would-be performer, so do not waste such a chance by being too passive or uninspiring in your approach.

However, aim to keep the balance by always respecting and giving time to the input of all the others too. Take the lead if and where appropriate but always make sure that you do so with the support of your fellows and, if you do find yourself instigating certain ideas, try to use this as an opportunity to draw others in rather than shut them out. There is nothing wrong with being seen as a leader in this type of situation, as long as it is respectful and constructive leadership that is on display. When appropriate, let others take the lead and follow and develop their input as you allowed others to do with yours.

A TYPICAL WORKSHOP AUDITION

Clearly there are any number of ways in which a workshop audition could progress and an array of possible content, limited only by the imagination of the organizers. However, it is a reasonably safe bet that it will begin with some physical and vocal warm-up, followed by some games to break down the participants' inhibitions and get them used to working with each other, and then some major exercise – usually to be completed in groups and perhaps performed to the whole group towards the end. It is not unusual either for a workshop

Accept and build

As much of the work undertaken in a workshop audition will be improvisational in approach, it will help you to remember this basic rule for improvisation generally: accept what you are given by your fellow performers (do not negate what they say or reject ideas that they inject into the work) and then build upon them (run with them and develop them further – adding to their depth and exploring their possibilities). This rule, applied specifically to exercises and generally throughout the workshop as a whole, will enable you to find the right balance and be a worthy participant without becoming overbearing.

to include some individual work (perhaps audition pieces) to be performed to everybody else at some stage during the proceedings. The amount of singing and dance content will, of course, depend on the nature of the job on offer.

The length of this type of audition can vary enormously. Sometimes they can last just a couple of hours but half- or even whole-day auditions are not unusual. They will certainly last longer than a normal audition and (more importantly) will demand of you a higher level of commitment and involvement. Because of this latter point, failure in a workshop audition can seem even more demoralizing than usual. As always, a positive attitude is the key here: look upon the event as a chance to explore and develop your skills. Remember that in the course of your career you will probably pay to attend various types of workshops for your professional development. Therefore, view these auditions as free opportunities to hone your skills, have some fun, meet and work with fellow performers, and make some new contacts. If you get the job too then that will be a very pleasing bonus!

A specific workshop audition is outlined below, to give a reasonably authentic idea of the kind of situation you can expect to encounter. It is written as if it were a planning document compiled by a workshop leader, and includes some advice in places to help you along the way. If you are in contact with a group of people similarly interested in the process of auditioning, you may wish to get together with them and actually try working through it for real. If you do this, make sure that you elect a leader, so that the experience remains focused and positive.

In order to encompass as many different types of performers as possible, this is a composite workshop, made up of many different elements to include voice, movement, singing, dancing, interaction, improvisation, devising, emotional work and children's theatre. Thus, although you may never attend such a wide-ranging audition, it will give you a general overview of the process.

We will imagine that this is an audition workshop with the purpose of casting a season of plays that will include a range of comedy and more serious plays, a musical play for children, and some Shakespeare. As such, an equally wide range of performers has been invited to attend, probably with specialities in certain areas, but general abilities in all of them as well.

Although a real workshop audition might include individual performances of acting pieces and/or songs to the group, this one does not.

Workshop games are fun and team building.

WORKSHOP

INTRODUCTIONS

Everyone is asked to sit in a circle and, briefly and in turn, is asked to say their name and a few words about themselves. They then stand and a ball is thrown around the circle – the name of the catcher being called out by the thrower.

WARM UP

This could take many different forms but would include voice, movement and singing.

GAME 1: PING, PANG, PONG

The leader starts by clapping their hands towards anyone else in the circle (except those on either side) and loudly saying *Pang*. This person (and subsequent players) claps towards another member but with the following rules attached to their vocal exclamation: for those on either side you must say *Ping*; for all others you must say *Pang*. You can send either of these back to the 'thrower' by clapping and then throwing your hands up as if in surrender and saying *Pong*. The sender must then redirect to another person with a *Ping* or a *Pang* – they cannot *Pong* a *Pong*! In addition a receiver can elect to shout the words together – *Ping, Pang, Pong* – and this means that the circle must disintegrate, with participants running around to other places to re-form it quickly. The person who ends up in the *Ping, Pang, Pong*-er's position must continue from there. The object of the game is for the group to work as a team to keep the action moving quickly, smoothly and without hesitation or mistake – if any of these happen the leader starts again.

GAME 2: HAND SLAP MURDER

Each member of the group puts both hands behind their back. They are instructed to place palms facing up. Everyone moves around the room. They must keep moving and must not stand with their backs to the wall. They can only remove hands from behind them momentarily and in order to try to slap one of the palms of another participant. If a hand is slapped it is removed from behind the back and the participant has lost a life. When both lives are lost they are out and leave the floor. The game promotes balanced movement and concentration as each member of the group tries to focus upon slapping and not being slapped at the same time. Towards the end of the game, participants can gang up upon individuals in order to corner them and remove them from the game. The last two standing can face a stalemate situation but this can be resolved if one 'rushes' the other, causing them to turn and flee – thus exposing themselves to being slapped before they can find room and time to turn to face their opponent again. Last standing is the winner.

GAME 3: ACTING MURDER

The group stands in a circle with eyes closed. The leader moves behind them and touches one of them silently upon the shoulder – they become the Secret Murderer. Players are told to open their eyes and can now move freely around the room. The Secret Murderer must attempt to touch another participant upon their arm or shoulder without the others seeing. If this is done successfully the victim must count to five (in order to give the Secret Murderer time to escape the immediate scene) and then die with a dramatic flourish. Anyone can accuse another of being the Secret Murderer after each murder. If they are right they are the winners and the game restarts; if wrong they are out of the game and it continues. The Secret Murderer wins if he or she claims a certain number of victims without identification – perhaps three.

GAME 4: MEMORY BALL

Again the group stands in a circle. They must throw the ball to each other randomly but call out the intended catcher's name as they do so. The leader allows this to continue for some time but instructs the participants to attempt to remember the sequence. When everyone has thrown and caught at least two times the sequence is restarted and players have to try to throw and catch in the same order – repeating the sequence exactly. This game promotes concentration but also encourages the group to think logically and throw in a pattern that they can remember easily.

EXERCISE 1: UNPREPARED IMPROVISATION

Pairs of players stand around the room. Each pair has an 'A' person and a 'B' person. The leader outlines a very simple, but potentially dramatic or comic scene – making clear the roles to be played by both A and B. On the word 'Go' the pairs must improvise this scene and do so without too much hesitation, ensuring that they advance the plot forward towards some kind of conclusion. All pairs are working at the same time, so there will be a general hubbub of sound and movement. After a minute (or alternative time limit decided by the leader) the scene is stopped and the As are asked to progress round the room to the next B and the process is repeated with another scene. This continues until all As have worked with all Bs. If there is an odd number in the group it simply means that a different B will be without a partner each time – and they can sit out for that scene.

This exercise creates a chaotic feeling of fun, loosens the imagination and gets everyone working and talking with each other quickly and effectively.

Two possible scenarios:

A has found an envelope, stuffed with bank notes, in the street. B thinks that they should take it to the police but A wants to keep it. How is the argument resolved?

B is convinced that A is someone famous, whom they recognize. Although A is not that person, B is irritatingly persistent in wanting their autograph.

EXERCISE 2: MOVEMENT

The group is asked to walk steadily around the room in a circle with relaxed but upright posture and keeping well balanced and centred in their movement. They are then asked to start leading with their heads. After they have done this for a while the leader instructs them to use the feeling of this to infect the rest of their bodies and turn them into some kind of character. After a while this is stopped and the process is repeated using chests, hips, knees and then feet – each time a new character is created. The movement around the room continues without pause throughout.

EXERCISE 3: VOICE

The group sits in a circle. Participants must close their eyes and promise to keep them closed throughout. The leader leads one of them silently and secretly into the centre of the circle (some loud music can be played momentarily to aid the secrecy). Players now take turns to ask the chosen one questions. She or he must disguise their voice by assuming an outlandish character and invent silly answers to the questions. They continue until someone successfully guesses who they are – or not.

EXERCISE 4: PREPARED IMPROVISATION

The group is split up into smaller groups of, say, three or four. Each group is asked to invent the title of a scene – this must be either potentially dramatic or comic but should not be too outlandish. This title is then given to the next group around the room – thus each group has a title that is not of their own devising. The groups are then asked to discuss and rehearse a scene with this title and are give their own area of space in which to do this.

Song and dance is often an important part of a workshop audition.

After a time limit – perhaps ten minutes – each group performs to all the others.

EXERCISE 5: DEVISING

The groups should now be reconstituted by swapping members around. Each group is then given a well-known fairy tale – say Little Red Riding Hood or Cinderella. They are then asked to drama-tize this within a set time limit – at least twenty or thirty minutes if time will allow. Again, it is then performed to the others. The groups should be encouraged to be as inventive as possible within this process – using their voices and movement imaginatively and without inhibition. It should be made clear to them that they can even use their bodies to create scenery and their voices for sound effects when appropriate. Members of the group can play more than one character and everything should be big, bold and colourful!

EXERCISE 6: SHAKESPEARE

The groups are reconstituted yet again. They are then given a copy of the Witches' scene from Macbeth, which they are asked to dramatize and perform – if time allows. This should be done as imaginatively as possible. (There is no reason why men should not play the witches here.)

SONG AND DANCE ENDING

The group is taught a show song around the piano. This should be a reasonably short song or a section of a longer one. They are then taken on to the floor and are taught dance moves to go with it – finishing with a complete run-through to end the session. This should all be done with energy and fun and should give the participant a chance to relax and let go, as well as demonstrate their musical skills.

10 Triumph and disaster

If you can dream – and not make dreams your master,
If you can think – and not make thoughts your aim,
If you can meet with Triumph and Disaster
And treat those two impostors just the same
…

Rudyard Kipling

DEALING WITH REJECTION AND MOVING FORWARD

In the spirit of treating the two impostors of triumph and disaster just the same, we will deal with disaster first, discussing ways to defuse it and make it positive, and then move on to glory in triumph!

THE ONLY CERTAINTY

A life in the professional theatre holds many uncertainties. There is very little job security (if any), no permanence, no structure and no consistency in any element of the performer's existence. To be fair, it is for these very reasons that many are attracted to the business in the first place – masochistic as they may be! Indeed the secure

and ordered world of a career in, say, a large bank contains only repugnant terror for most thespians, singers and dancers.

However, there is one irrefutable certainty for all performers – one that will haunt the lives of all exponents of theatrical pursuits however hard they try to avoid it – and that is rejection. Rejection is a major part of every career, and those who cannot become used to it and cope with its extreme negativity will perish long before they taste any kind of success at all.

We have already explored how rejection can play an important part in the vocation testing process and how degrees of it can help measure and structure movement towards the goal of, perhaps, obtaining a place at an accredited drama school or college. But rejection is not confined to the beginnings of careers – it is always prevalent. Neither will it easily be tamed into a positive force, preferring instead to apply its negativity relentlessly throughout the working lifetime of a performer without any recourse to fairness, controllability or purpose.

Neither does rejection limit itself to one incarnation: it springs up in many forms and intensities, ranging from the simple disregard of an application letter carefully penned, through never hearing back about an audition at which you thought you had performed well, to not getting a wonderful job in the West End of London after six recalls and being whittled down eventually to 'the last two'. The degrees of heartache that it can impose are endless and eternal, and even in the most

OPPOSITE: Rejection is always personal, but you must remain positive.

successful careers it will, having 'played dead', suddenly resurrect itself to bring a long held part in, for example, a television soap to an abrupt and painful end.

Personal rejection

Part of the problem of rejection is the nature of the art form that you are (or want to be) involved in. For instance, if a painter has her or his work rejected by a gallery then as hard as this may be for them it is, at least, only their work that has been spurned not them personally. But a performer does not use paint and canvas as their tools of the trade or materials – they use their own voices and bodies. In having their talent rejected, they face the rejection of their very selves too. This makes the hardship even more acute and generally depressing.

A SOLUTION?

It is certainly possible to have a strategy for rejection and part of this strategy is to be realistic about it. Realistic, not just in the sense of acknowledging it, but also in the sense of honestly appraising its frequency and effect upon your standard of life.

For instance, if all you experience is rejection over a long period of time, without any success at all to break or dilute the agony, then it can sometimes be useful to listen to what this might be telling you. There comes a time in every career, at what ever stage, when enough is enough and it is better to retire the 'field of battle' gracefully. Yes, perseverance and dedication are essential, and so is the ability to endure hardship and not give up easily. However, not to give up at all, when you are perhaps no longer enjoying what once motivated and inspired you, is foolhardy, reckless and pointless.

But we are talking about extreme and unrelenting, long-term rejection here. Your strategy must also encompass the ordinary, workaday, regular but not totally insuperable rejection too. In the short term it is most certainly not necessary to allow failure to beat you, and you must fortify yourself against its acidic properties at all costs.

Although you cannot make rejection in itself positive – you cannot somehow magically convert its darkening presence to sunlight – you can at least counter it with a positive action to match it.

THE 'TIT FOR TAT' STRATEGY

Every time you experience any type of rejection you will feel despondent and low. However, even though you may feel defeated in the short term, you must act immediately for the good of the long term.

Therefore, for every piece of rejection you encounter you should take counter-action with three particular measures:

1. Make yourself feel better by giving yourself a treat. This is not the most professional of the measures but it works, at least to some extent. The treat can suit your budget: a cup of your favourite coffee with a friend to console and cheer you in your refreshment establishment of choice will suffice if necessary.
2. In accordance with general advice elsewhere in this book, write to the management concerned and thank them for the audition and ask to be considered for further opportunities. Then make a note to contact them again in the future. Remember this important fact: rejection does not necessarily equal total

OPPOSITE: **You must be strong, for your theatrical journey will not be an easy one.**

failure, as even a negative result now may still have opened a door for later on – provided you stick your foot in it!

3. Do one special thing to obtain more work. This can be anything: writing a letter, sending a CV, making a phone call. The specifics here are not important – it is the discipline of the action that counts. However, make sure that it is in addition to any normal work-finding activity you would normally do that day and link it in your mind specifically with the rejection experience.

GETTING THE PART AND BEYOND

Although you will have to cope with rejection in order to survive, as a professional performer you will need to learn how to deal with success as well as failure. This is not quite as easy as you might think; in fact, obtaining work is only the first step and can prove to be the easy bit!

OPENING DOORS

Having obtained a job you will, or should be, delighted. It is almost certain that you will have put more physical, cerebral and emotional effort into obtaining it than a member of any other profession would have done to obtain a single short-term contract. You will have written, followed up, prepared for auditions and recalls, have worried, hoped and dreamed – and finally, at much cost, the job will be yours. However, elated as you are, the hard fact is that this will be just one job. However hard you may have worked to attain this job, however much of yourself you have invested in pursuing it, however long a contract it may be, you will not have secured your career for life but simply have secured one small victory in a long and difficult war. This of course will be irrelevant at the time, and your victory will be sweet but, in the long term, it is a small part of a much wider strategy.

This may be a depressing and, perhaps, nega-

tive thought but it points you firmly towards the importance of how well you perform in this particular job – not just in terms of your talent but in your conduct as an employee too. It is very unlikely that the company who have awarded you this job are undertaking this project in total isolation: they will probably have mounted such projects in the past and, more importantly, will be doing so in the future. Indeed, they will, like you, be aiming 'upwards and outwards' – intent on developing their profile and importance within the industry. Therefore this job must be viewed as not just a single opportunity but a precious chance to prove that you are a potential prospect for further and continued employment.

The whole of your career is going to be about 'opening doors' – establishing yourself within a theatre company or arts organization as a talented, useful and reliable actor. Most theatrical employers would admit (if they were honest) that they would rather cast someone they know than go through the arduous and risky procedure of auditioning new prospects – especially if they have left the casting until late (as often happens). Therefore, 'opening doors' in this way is the very structuring of your career itself: a lifetime of endless casting processes to secure single opportunities of employment would be exhausting and demoralizing – each one must be viewed as a new beginning; a new chance to add yet another employment stream to your long-term future. As these build up, so you will begin to rely more and more on your reputation and establishment as an actor and less and less on individual auditions. Thus, each new casting will become the prospect of yet another layer of employment and not just single opportunities. This attitude will give you a much more positive outlook, both practically and emotionally.

CLOSING DOORS

In the same way a door can be opened, so it can be closed: theatrical productions are high-risk operations for producers, whether they be commercial or funded, and they will naturally want to employ people who are not only talented but reliable. It is worth pointing out that, as vulnerable and artistic beings, directors will want to work with people they can trust on both a practical and emotional level. If any of these vital aspects are missing from your 'portfolio' during your first job with any producer or director then it is likely to be your last job for them too – and this, unless you don't enjoy working for them for any reason (they need to cultivate you as a long-term prospect too, remember), will be counter-productive to your career as a 'jobbing actor'.

The next section of this chapter looks at some of the important ways in which a performer should conduct themselves in order to make themselves a truly useful member of the team and worthy of future and continued employment. Before this, however, it is essential to point out that you must not confuse making yourself employable in an ongoing way with allowing yourself to be taken advantage of or treated in an unacceptable manner. If you have serious issues with an organization that you are working for and feel that they are acting in a way that is not within the bounds of either your contract or acceptable practice, then you should politely stand up for yourself regardless of any unfair damage this may do to your reputation. In other words, if a company isn't worthy of your services now they are not worthy of them in the future either – so don't mistake diligence for uncritical compliance.

PUNCTUALITY

There is one simple rule for a performer in terms of being late for work – don't be – ever! This may seem rather harsh and uncompromising and, admittedly, it might not always be possible to adhere to absolutely. However, as an attitude of mind, it is essential.

In the modern world generally there has steadily developed an acceptance of poor punctuality: many people, and indeed organizations, have begun to believe that being late is acceptable – regrettable rather than disastrous – something one tries to avoid but cannot be blamed for if it happens. Do not be fooled into thinking this attitude now exists too in theatre, because it most certainly doesn't! Obviously being late for a performance is bad news (and missing a half-hour call totally unacceptable), but so is being late for a rehearsal or any other type of call. As has already been established, theatrical productions, be they stage, television or film, are financially and artistically risky and hazardous enterprises – performers being late can cost time and money that is simply not affordable. Therefore make sure that it is very clear in your mind now that, in terms of your chosen vocation (and this word alone is a clue to your attitude) lateness does not exist – theatre does not 'do' late!

One of the problems for the modern performer is that the atmosphere of theatrical companies does not help in keeping punctuality ever-mindful. Theatre people are, by and large, very affable people and everyone (vulnerable and insecure as they may feel) is anxious to remain friendly and to avoid unnecessary confrontation with people whose support and comradeship are essential for their own artistic security. This is of course a good thing and one of the reasons why working in theatre is such a rewarding and privileged experience. However, it does mean that lateness will rarely promote an aggressive or even tangible reaction – it is unlikely that a latecomer will be 'told off' in any way. Unfortunately, lack of discernible judgement does not mean that it will not exist and lateness will always be secretly noted (albeit subconsciously) by colleagues and, more importantly, directors – and repeated lateness will be resented. It is a sobering fact that the performers who hold up proceedings are not the ones who secure further employment – however admirable they may be in other areas of their competency.

Because of this it is important that you have, from the start, your own personal policy in place regarding punctuality. Your practical strategies in this area are simple: get up earlier than you need to and get an earlier train or (if driving) beat the rush hour. Most importantly, take personal responsibility for your timekeeping. Remember that the person who drives your train or bus is an employed person with job security – you are not – so it is no good blaming them.

HEALTH

As a professional performer, try to keep as healthy as possible – both in the long and short term. Many productions that you will be involved in will not have sufficient budgetary resilience to deal with members of the cast missing from either performances or rehearsals. Although there will be times when unavoidable illness or indisposition will mean that you are unable to continue, you must take every precaution possible to avoid this. Keep fit and healthy generally and, when working, try to protect yourself from infections as much as possible. Pantomimes and other Christmas shows are notorious for experiencing outbreaks of colds and 'flu amongst their companies. A small but effective precaution is to tour your own mug – washing up in theatrical organizations is not always as thorough as it might be and this is a common way in which germs can spread.

Remember that if you do need to take time off, the turmoil that this causes will ultimately reflect on you – however unfair and consciously unintentional this may be. If you do have to absent yourself through illness do not take this lightly and make sure that the management understands how seriously you view the situation. Also make sure

OPPOSITE: **You should keep good time and never be late.**

that if you can keep going you do. Obviously don't put your long-term health in danger but resort to absence only as a last resort.

A POSITIVE AND SUPPORTIVE ATTITUDE

When you are working it will not be necessary for you to be sycophantic towards the management and the director (in fact, this is the one thing that you should never be), but it is important that you are positive towards the production and its company members and that you take a supportive interest in its success. This may seem very obvious advice, but theatrical productions of every kind can be stressful and difficult at times and it is easy for problems and irritations to get out of proportion and steer you towards negativity. Sometimes, things might be so bad that this is inevitable (although you will find this very rare in the profession), but usually you will discover that keeping a level head will help you not to let small setbacks get out of proportion. If you are the one to remain positive in the face of difficulty then others will follow and you will have played your part in creating a supportive and united company.

Likewise, do not take issue with the management over things that are not important: however much right may be on your side it is not worth alienating yourself and jeopardizing future employment for the sake of fighting trivial causes. Of course, you should complain and be outspoken if you have to, but make sure that it is necessary – theatrical managements and directors are under a lot of pressure too. Again, think about the 'door' – you should not close it without good cause!

WORK HARD

This may seem like very obvious advice but there are some professional performers who do not work hard enough – especially during and prior to rehearsals. Always make sure that you do your homework before the start of the rehearsal process. It may be necessary for you to pre-learn at

Work breeds more work and a career can slowly build.

least some of the lines, depending upon how long you actually have to rehearse. However, at the very least, you should read the play thoroughly, and have begun to be familiar with what you will have to say and do.

If you are fortunate enough to have a long rehearsal period do not postpone your homework upon the script. Make sure that you learn the lines thoroughly and steadily and do not leave this process too late. Although you do not want to rush the assimilation process, it will not look good if, towards the latter stages of rehearsal, all of the cast are 'off book' except for you.

Similarly, take performances seriously even if you have only a small part to play. Make sure that you warm up the voice, body and mind in a way that you find useful and appropriate, and be as focused as possible. Remember that performing is very much a team effort, and you will not want to be the one who lets the others down.

Working is an opportunity

We have already examined how vital it is that you should make a good impression upon your employers, thus encouraging them to use you again. But it is also vital to use the opportunity to advertise your skills to other potential employers. Always make sure that you target and contact as many of these as possible and invite them to a performance. If you are looking for an agent this is of particular use, as many agents are reluctant to take on new clients if they have not seen them work.

   Although you will not find this process easy and, obviously, it will be even more difficult if you are working away from London or other central cities in the world, it must be done. Many performers say that they are too busy rehearsing the play and learning the lines to do this, but do it they must if they are at all hopeful of building an established career. Do not miss the opportunity that working affords you to promote yourself. Similarly, if you know a manager, director or agent has seen a performance that you have been involved with, contact them in order to introduce yourself – there is no better way of initiating a contact than by having your work seen.

11 The amateur alternative

A HOBBY FOR LIFE

Much of this book, especially the early part, has been concerned with the necessity for you to test your vocation; to make sure, before you commit yourself to a life of perpetual professional auditions (in which you are statistically more likely to fail than to succeed), that you are fully suited, in terms of talent, dedication and temperament, to such a demanding and unforgiving existence.

One of the hard facts of any such examination of your vocation is that the honest answer may be 'no'. (Of course, it may be 'yes' and, if this is the case, you will proceed with assurance.) Part of the reason for such testing in the first place is to allow you to pursue alternative strategies if necessary. You may not be destined for a professional career doing the thing that you love, but you do not necessarily have to abandon it. On the contrary, once you have determined that, despite your great love of performing (straight or musical), the professional route is not for you, then not only will you be liberated to discover another career with which you have an affinity, but you can also

OPPOSITE: A supportive ensemble is extremely important.

dedicate yourself to an equally rewarding amateur career as a performer at the same time.

AMATEUR EXCELLENCE

There was perhaps a time in the past when the phrase 'amateur theatre' would conjure up an image of draughty church halls, wobbly (not to say collapsing) scenery, excruciatingly bad acting to the point of the comedic, endless prompting from the wings (often the prompter having more to say than anyone in the cast), characters entering through the fireplace because the door is stuck, and the vicar's wife playing a part for which she is at least twenty years too old! However, times have changed. Although there are still amateur companies that remain endearingly dubious in their abilities, there are many now that present a very different image indeed.

To begin with, many amateur companies now present their productions in proper theatres that are hired for the purpose, sometimes at considerable expense. This affords the performers (and the audience) a much more satisfying and rewarding experience. In addition, they are far more discerning about membership and casting – thus the standard of performance is much higher. Direction is far better too, along with production values and budgetary investment generally – all adding to the prospect of a satisfying and worthwhile dedication to a part-time, voluntary and lifelong experience.

AUDITIONING FOR AMATEUR COMPANIES

One of the revolutions in amateur theatre is the way in which productions are now often cast. In the past everything was very much centred around the particular 'society' to which you belonged. Each club or society would have its own membership and all of the personnel for every production (front and back stage) would be assembled from within these ranks. Although a few adventurous theatricals would belong to more than one club, the majority stayed loyal to one and would wait hopefully and expectantly to be selected for juicy roles in the shows as they occurred throughout the calendar. Those with the most experience tended to get the best parts.

These days many clubs now model themselves upon a more professional blueprint. They think of themselves as 'companies' rather than 'clubs' and mount their productions as independent entities. Rather than relying on an ever-circulating and stagnating membership list for casting, they hold open auditions, to which any and all of the local amateur theatre 'community' are welcome to attend and put themselves forward for parts. The casts are then assembled from the best and most suitable performers available, whether or not they are members of the particular company in question. If they are given a part and are not members they may be required to join, meaning that membership becomes something of a technicality rather than a matter of individual loyalty. In a way this is a shame, as much of the identity and

camaraderie of individual societies has been lost but, on the positive side, it means that the hobby has become far more structured as a whole and can be pursued in a more satisfying way for those who wish to take the activity seriously and establish themselves as 'jobbing' amateur performers rather than just members of a drama club.

So the process of seeking roles is now not too dissimilar from professional theatre. However, there is an essential difference that probably makes things, if anything, slightly trickier: whereas professionals (or their agents) will submit a letter, CV and photograph, amateur auditions tend to be 'open' and directors make their selections from those who turn up on the day (or evening). This means that there is not so much of a concentration upon particular parts and the director will be looking at a variety of possibilities and combinations of casting from the performers who present themselves. Therefore, although participants may suggest themselves for the role upon which their heart is set, they are likely to end up with another. Although this kind of compromise can be disappointing, it does at least mean that total rejection is not always the order of the day if one particular part cannot be secured.

This important factor means that you will need a very specific attitude to life on the amateur circuit: not only will you need to be flexible in terms of which parts you believe you are suited to, you will also need to be prepared and ready for anything. You may well attend an audition with a special role in mind but then have to 'read' for another or several others. In this respect you will need to be versatile, not only when performing but when auditioning also.

Something else to remember is that the open nature of many of these auditions means that you may well have a selection of other performers to work with and 'bounce off' when you are reading the script, and this will prove a helpful and natural approach. You may also find that the director

OPPOSITE: An amateur 'career' need not be 'second best'.

Assess the play and yourself when preparing for an audition.

will actually run or work on scenes with movement – making full use of the communal nature of the audition and giving you a good chance to demonstrate your skills.

PREPARING FOR THE AUDITION

When you are preparing for an audition you will need a very good working knowledge of the play as a whole and of all of the characters. You will also need to assess the parts for which you are suitable and concentrate even more upon those. In doing this you must be both imaginative and realistic: imaginative in envisaging how you could play a role effectively and in a way that would work even if you were not absolutely ideal in age or type, for example; and realistic – knowing which parts would be entirely beyond the realms of your suitability, however enticing they might appear.

EXERCISE: PREPARING A PLAY FOR AUDITION

This exercise can be used for a real audition using the play in question or a fictitious one using a play of your choosing.

1. Obtain a copy of the play. If you are selecting this for the purpose of the exercise, make sure that it is one that contains a reasonable number of parts. It can be either comedy or straight but, for the purpose of the exercise, it should not be too unusual, hard-hitting or controversial. It should be of good quality, by a recognized playwright, and one that might be a popular choice for an amateur company playing to a variety of different people. You should buy the script rather than borrow it from a library so that you can freely make notes upon it. You can buy good-quality secondhand copies of most plays cheaply and easily on the Internet.

2. Read the play through thoroughly and carefully. Make sure that you have a good grasp of the plot and of its themes and ideas. Make notes in pencil as you go along, highlighting any aspects of the play that you find interesting or challenging and which may be a possible focus for exploration in either an audition or in the rehearsal process.

3. Select the characters that you feel are within the scope of your casting potential. For the exercise in particular you can use a wide remit – even considering 'ageing-up' possibilities if they are reasonably realistic. Make detailed notes about each of them and detail your impressions of them as people. In doing this, think not only about their personalities but also their physical and vocal characteristics. Be as indulgent as you wish and build up an in-depth picture for each character.

4. Now read the play out loud, playing all of the different parts yourself. It will be fun to do this for the play in its entirety but, if you do not have the time or will for this, you can select the scenes that contain the most characters that are applicable to you. It is important that you approach this in a slightly exaggerated manner – going just a little 'over the top' for the sake of full character exploration at this stage, but avoiding trivialization. This will help you to experiment with the various character voices and will enable you to get a feel for how the characters relate to each other. Enjoy playing around with rhythm, pace and modulation.

5. Repeat at least some of the scenes in a similar way but, this time, stand up and move about in a very rough approximation of how the scene might be blocked (what moves and where). If your own living space is approximate to the setting you can use this for added realism. You will now be getting a feel for the way in which the character moves as well as speaks and you can be equally experimental in this.

AT THE AUDITION

Having done this careful preparation, you must apply it successfully at the audition. As has already been said, it will probably be a communal affair with lots of people watching others audition while they await their turn. It is also likely that different scenes will be read with different combinations of cast, so most people will stay for the duration of the evening. The scenes will probably be moved as well as read, with performers constantly getting up and down to participate when required. There will be a great deal of milling about and general chit-chat while the proceedings unfold. Although such an energized atmosphere can be great fun and promote a sense of community, it can also

Ongoing development

Once you have started to get regular parts and have begun to establish yourself on your local amateur scene, make sure that you consolidate and develop your skills with an ongoing programme of personal development. You should think about going to classes (either private or group) to improve and extend your technique, read as much as possible (plays and books about theatre and performing), and generally immerse yourself in the hobby. After all, if something is worthy of being part of your life and experience at all, then it should be done well and with as much investment of your time and commitment as you are able to give.

If you are expecting to be able to access much of this development from the group(s) to which you belong, you may be disappointed: although many amateur theatre companies see the benefit of education and development, and actively encourage and organize it within their society, a great many others do not. Unfortunately, many clubs feel that their reason for existence is to produce shows and that any further engagement with the craft, generally or specifically, is not necessary. This is a great shame as they, and their members, are missing out on much of the interest, excitement and joy of the hobby.

There are several reasons why this state of affairs prevails in many amateur theatre societies. It is partly apathy or lack of time and commitment, but there are other reasons too. Unfortunately, there are individuals and groups who feel that they do not need to learn any more and that ongoing training would not only be superfluous but demeaning. (Training and tuition is often offered by local professionals, or by teachers who are also professional performers, and this can exacerbate a defensive attitude from amateurs towards the profession.)

Part of the solution is to initiate and pursue your own programme of development. There will be many opportunities for you to attend classes and take part in workshops – especially if you live near a big city – and you should take advantage of these regularly, as well as visiting the theatre as often as you can and keeping up your reading and personal study. The Internet and your local library are good sources of information about local opportunities.

However, you should also consider proactively encouraging your group to follow your example. If they do not run regular workshops, for instance, encourage them to do so or, better still, persuade them to let you run them yourself. Try to initiate a programme of regular development sessions. These can be based around the current production in rehearsal or more generally relevant to the craft, and you should try to engage the services of a number of different teachers and practitioners who might be able to afford an insight into the many different aspects of drama and its execution. For example, a workshop on Restoration comedy and its techniques can be great fun, as well as being outside the normal experience of some performers, and there are enough possibilities for other sessions to keep your company regularly stimulated on an ongoing basis.

Although you may encounter some resistance at first, persevere – for you will be doing your colleagues a great service in the end and one that may completely revolutionize their appreciation and enjoyment of performing. After all, many other hobbies encompass some tuition as a matter of course. A golfer, for instance, would think nothing of having a regular lesson with the club professional (provided they can afford it), and a photographic society would engage regular speakers to interest and educate their members.

Ongoing development is the key to success, and a keen amateur should always look for learning opportunities.

be potentially intimidating – especially for someone who has not auditioned for the particular company before and doesn't know anyone else in the room.

The advice in this case is to throw caution to the wind and get fully involved from the start. Introduce yourself to others, chat to as many people as possible (although not when it might be disturbing the proceedings of course), take great enjoyment in playing the various scenes and try to make your enthusiasm infectious so that you will naturally encourage the others to do the same. Although you should be careful to avoid becoming overbearing, you should give and confirm the impression that you are likely to be a positive and a fully contributing company member who will bring energy and commitment to the project. This will, of course, stand you in good stead for the future as well as for this particular production.

As you work upon the scenes, make sure that you are fully engaged with the material. If the director gives you some direction, listen carefully, assimilate it and then try to 'run with it' energetically and imaginatively. There are no prizes for caution in the theatre world (amateur or professional) and you must take chances here in order to fulfil your potential and, it is hoped, win the approval of the director and production team. Have fun and play around with the material as you did at home, feeling confident that you have talent and ability that is worth showing off. After this it is up to them to decide if they want you, but at least you will have given them plenty of information about yourself and your work to enable them to make the decision. It is far better to be noticed and fail than to fail because you have not been noticed!

THE LONG HAUL

In terms of the rehearsal schedule, amateur theatre follows a very different pattern by necessity. Whilst professional performers are having to get used to ever-shorter rehearsal periods, those amongst the amateur ranks will need to set their preparation clock somewhat differently. Rehearsals will usually take place upon one or two evenings each week at the most, and probably last for only around two to three hours. As the opening of the production approaches this will probably increase and there is usually a full weekend of technical and dress rehearsals prior to the performance week. However, in general, the progress of preparation will be slow and measured.

Although this has the advantage of allowing a reasonably stress-free and relaxed approach to the show, it does also mean that you will need to keep your interest, focus and inspiration strong and unwavering over quite a long period of time within the calendar. You must also guard against complacency and prevarication, and make the most of the opportunity to work slowly and methodically, rather than succumbing to the temptation to defer work (especially line-learning) because you feel you have too much time. You will completely negate the advantages of such a long rehearsal period if you put things off until the last minute.

SHORT AND SWEET

In contrast to the long period of preparation, the show itself is usually conducted over a very short period of time and a limited number of performances. A week of six or seven shows is usually the longest run of any production and some companies will perform for just three nights at the end of the week. This will inevitably be frustrating for, as enjoyable and immensely satisfying the experience of performing should be, the shortness of its lifespan will always feel disappointing and anticlimactic after so long and arduous a build-up. It does, however, have the advantage of throwing the focus upon the quality of preparation and development of actors' skills. The rehearsal process should therefore be viewed not just as a means to an end – the performances – but rather as something intrinsically worthwhile and enriching. The very nature of the imbalance leads to this conclusion and yet, strangely, drama clubs do not always fully appreciate and take advantage of this.

Guard against complacency and prevarication!

12 Being a performing arts student

AN END AND A BEGINNING

If you are already something of an experienced professional and your purpose in reading this book has been to improve your auditioning technique and job-finding skills, then you may wish to ignore this short chapter, which is primarily aimed at those whose agenda is to find a place at drama school or other performing arts establishment.

If you are talented, resolved and (to an extent) lucky enough to secure a place, it will help you to take a brief glimpse at what awaits you. Certainly, the journey so far will not have been an easy one, and if you have been invited to join a course at an accredited drama school, then your effort and achievement will have undoubtedly been high.

BE PREPARED

Unfortunately, this is only the beginning of your struggles, for completing a professional performer's course of any worth involves a great deal of hard work and high-pressure self development. This is not to put you off, as the rewards and satisfaction that await you are immense. A common (if mistaken) view of student life, especially in the first year, is that of relaxation and 'partying'. This

OPPOSITE: **A theatrical career is all about 'opening doors' and then keeping them open.**

has no truth whatsoever in terms of vocational actor and musical theatre training. You must be prepared to be dedicated and hard-working from the very first day, and you must also be ready for an extraordinary and intense experience.

This type of training usually focuses upon taking the various elements of a student's 'performing instrumentation' apart (metaphorically, of course), moulding and sculpting it, and then putting it back together again. Many feel that the process makes them a new person as well as a new performer (usually in a positive way), but such drastic and complex reconstruction comes at a price. There are some for whom the journey becomes too demanding and the drop-out rate is high. However, for those who are prepared and able to make the effort needed, the reward is an ability to enter the profession with a strong chance (albeit not a guarantee) of success in one of the toughest jobs in the world.

Previous advice about your conduct when working, especially time-keeping, is just as important here. You will be expected not only to be dedicated and self-disciplined but resilient and resourceful as well. The hours will be long (particularly when you are rehearsing a show and continuing with your usual classes too) and the workload will be unrelenting. On top of this, if your tutors are working professionals (as many of them should be), they will not be inclined to show you any mercy in driving you towards what they know only too well to be a difficult goal.

BE OPEN

It will be necessary for you to be mentally open to new ideas and possibilities within yourself. Although you will not be expected to absorb your training without question or personal deliberation, you will need to show a general acceptance of the college's philosophy and methods, and be positive in your interactions with them. Having chosen the establishment that is right for you, and having persuaded them to choose you, you must now put your trust in the regime and really 'go with it'! Conflict with your tutors will be unproductive, so make sure that, while putting your point of view when appropriate, you remain very much a part of their team and ready to assimilate their wisdom proactively.

MAKE THE MOST OF IT

Having won a place on such a course at considerable expense, fully avail yourself of this opportunity and do not squander your time. If you are on a one-year course you will need to be even more diligent. What you will learn at drama school should stand you in good stead for the rest of your working life: it will be the very foundation of your future development and progress. If you are on a good course you will find yourself referencing what you have learned again and again over the years. In fact, you may often find that you suddenly and unexpectedly reach a full understanding of some technique or other which during your training seemed interesting but only now comes into focus. Because of all of this, you must see your time training as an investment of energy that will pay great dividends.

OPPOSITE: **Hard work and dedication are essential.**

In particular, make the most of your 'finals' – the last term(s) when you perform to the public. Ensure that you invite as many industry people to see you as possible – especially agents. This is your chance to get a good start and, although it will be difficult, there is nothing wrong with aiming to leave the course with representation and your first job secured. Think big – but be prepared to supply the hard work and dedication to make your dreams a reality.

PRACTICALITIES

There will be a certain amount of equipment that you will need – mainly books and dance and movement kit. The details of this will, of course, be supplied by the college before you begin. Although you will probably be on a tight budget, try not to economize with this too much and if possible make sure that you have all you need and that it is of reasonable quality.

If you need to stay away from home, try to find good accommodation that will be comfortable and homely. You will be there for quite a while and you will be working hard and under great pressure and, thus, it is essential that you have a welcoming place to return to. You may find it economical to share accommodation and this can often be a positive thing. However, try to ensure that you have your own space – both literally and metaphorically – so that you can, if possible, escape from the rigours of your existence at least occasionally. It will help to plan in advance, so begin investigating possibilities as soon as you can, rather than leaving it until just before your course starts to sort out your living arrangements.

WHAT TO EXPECT

The basic principles of most professional training courses are the same, although the particulars of the course will vary depending upon where you go. In order to give you an idea of what to expect, there follows a hypothetical example of a typical drama school course prospectus. For the sake of brevity and consolidation it takes the form of a one-year (possibly postgraduate) course. Although it is by no means a blueprint, it gives a basic indication of how such a course would intend to educate and train you for a life in the theatre.

This fictional course (very much in keeping with the ideas and philosophies of the author) is designed to operate within a working theatre. When choosing a drama school, you should look for established and proven courses that offer similar breadth and professionalism where possible.

Happy auditioning!

Course content

The course, which seeks to attain accreditation at the earliest opportunity, has the unique facility of operating within a working theatre with a solid reputation for in-house production and theatre arts education. Many of the components of the syllabus have been developed through first-hand experience of the needs of the modern professional. The course aims to marry a modern flexible approach (with a mind to the ever increasing emphasis on a more physical approach to theatre) with a re-emphasizing of some of the traditional skills and disciplines, which we feel should not be lost. We aim to produce actors who will be equally at home in a large-scale classical production, a commercial seaside repertory season, a modern studio show, or on television and radio. Blending these together will be a strong focus on developing actors with a positive and practical attitude towards obtaining work and a broad ability to work well and confidently within the framework of today's profession.

The course is intensive and deliberately reflects the working pressures likely to be encountered in the profession. Only those whom the Theatre considers to be definitely capable of pursuing a career as an actor in terms of both talent and dedication will be accepted on the course and their suitability will continue to be monitored and assessed throughout. Students will receive a report on their progress after each of the first two terms. This will be given by way of a short personal interview with each main subject tutor and the Course Director.

The course is practitioner-based and the various tutors are appointed from the ranks of experienced teachers within their particular fields and working professionals with extensive practical experience. In addition, all directors have the appropriate expertise related to the production or project assigned to them.

Term 1
- Extensive voice and movement training.
- Classes in period and character movement.
- Text interpretation.
- Verse speaking.

- Extensive acting classes with a wide and open-minded remit – teaching a broadly Stanislavski-based approach whilst also exploring the more stylized performance disciplines.
- Comedy technique.
- Stagecraft.
- Improvisation.
- Classes in stage combat (students work towards their Basic Fight Certificate at the end of the course).
- Stage Management, with specific attention devoted to the role of Assistant Stage Manager and to being 'on the book'.
- Basic grounding in the technical side of lighting and sound.
- Two acting projects for assessment: contemporary and Greek.

Term 2
- Movement work broadened to include Commedia and Mime.
- Radio Technique classes (students are entered for the Carleton Hobbs radio competition).
- Dialect tuition.
- Stage make-up classes.
- Audition technique.
- 'The Job of Acting' – weekly class focusing on professional discipline and general career management (taxation, advertising, photographs, CVs, etc.).
- Four practical projects: nineteenth century, Shakespeare, Restoration, and Television Contemporary (although at this stage television technique will be explored away from a television studio).
- Other disciplines continue and develop from Term 1.

Term 3
This is divided into two units.

Unit 1 (Weeks 1 to 6)
- Television tuition within a studio environment, leading to a filmed project from which a demonstration tape will be made for each student.
- Tuition classes continue and students are assessed.
- Physical Theatre and Mask Work classes.
- Theatre practitioners will lecture on a number of subjects, including various associated jobs (marketing, management, etc.).
- Theatre In Education project.
- Pantomime and Children's Theatre: techniques and conventions.
- 'Showcase', performed to an invited audience of managers and agents.
- Weekly tutorial, with appraisal of individual priorities for future development.

Unit 2 (Weeks 7 to 12) – Finals

- Rehearsal and presentation of two full-length plays in a fortnightly rep format. These are public performances with full technical and stage management support. Agents and managers will be invited to attend performances and after-show receptions will be arranged to give them the opportunity to meet students.
- Formal classes will cease but rehearsals will include limber sessions in both movement and voice.

Further reading

Berland, Terry, *Breaking Into Commercials: The Complete Guide to Marketing Yourself, Auditioning to Win, and Getting the Job* (Plume Books, 1997)

Bicat, Tina, and Baldwin, Chris (eds.), *Devised and Collaborative Theatre* (The Crowood Press, 2002)

Earley, Michael, and Keil, Philippa, *The Classical Monologue for Women* (Routledge, 1992)

Earley, Michael, and Keil, Philippa, *Soliloquy: Shakespeare Monologues for Men* (Applause Theatre Books, 1988)

Earley, Michael, and Keil, Philippa, *Soliloquy: Shakespeare Monologues for Women* (Applause Theatre Books, 1988)

Edwardes, Jane, *The Faber Book of Monologues for Men* (Faber and Faber, 2005)

Edwardes, Jane, *The Faber Book of Monologues for Women* (Faber and Faber, 2005)

Flom, Jonathan, *Get the Callback: The Art of Auditioning for Musical Theatre* (Scarecrow Press, 2009)

Harvey, Anne, *The Methuen Book of Monologues for Young Actors* (Methuen Drama, 2003)

Hester, John, *Stage Acting Techniques* (The Crowood Press, 2004)

Hester, John, *Understanding and Researching Scripts* (The Crowood Press, 2006)

Hester, John, *Performing Shakespeare* (The Crowood Press, 2008)

Hooks, Ed, *Ultimate Scene and Monologue Sourcebook, The Updated and Expanded Edition: An Actor's Guide to Over 1,000 Monologues and Scenes from More than 300 Contemporary Plays* (Watson-Guptill, revised edition 2007)

Marlow, Jean, *Audition Speeches for Young Actors* (A & C Black, 2002)

Perry, John, *The Rehearsal Handbook* (The Crowood Press, 2001)

Pierce, J.P., *Killer Monologues: Highly Actable Monologues and Performance Tips to Give You an Almost Unfair Advantage in the Auditioning Game* (Impact Films, 1998)

Ratliff, Gerald Lee, *The Theatre Audition Book 2: Playing Monologs from Contemporary, Modern, Period, Shakespeare and Classical Plays* (Meriwether, 2009)

See, Joan, *Acting in Commercials: Guide to Auditioning and Performing on Camera* (Back Stage Books, 1998)

Taylor, Millie, *Singing for Musicals* (The Crowood Press, 2008)

Index